T0265686

Preexisting Conditions

Wuhan, China, February 8, 2020 (Getty Images).

Preexisting Conditions

Recounting the Plague

Samuel Weber

ZONE BOOKS · NEW YORK

2022

The author wishes to express his extreme gratitude to the team at Zone Books who were decisive in turning a rough manuscript into a readable publication: Ramona Naddaff, Meighan Gale, Vanessa Davies, Joanna Steinhardt, Thomas Kozachek, and Julie Fry. It has been a pleasure working with them.

Distributed by Princeton University Press,
Princeton, New Jersey, and Woodstock, United Kingdom

Library of Congress Cataloging-in-Publication Data
Names: Weber, Samuel, 1940– , author.
Title: Preexisting conditions : recounting the plague / Samuel Weber.
Description: New York : Zone Books, 2022. | Includes bibliographical
     references and index. | Summary: "Plagues and pandemics
     confront societies with something they often seek to deny, namely
     that mortality and vulnerability is not just an individual concern.
     The narratives examined in this book both confirm the desire to
     avoid this recognition as well as the different ways it asserts itself
     nevertheless" — Provided by publisher.
Identifiers: LCCN 2021054586 | ISBN 9781942130765 (hardback) |
     ISBN 9781942130772 (ebook)
Subjects: LCSH: Epidemics — History. | Epidemics — Social aspects. |
     Narration (Rhetoric) | Epidemics in literature.
Classification: LCC RA649 .W2754 2022 | DDC 614.4/9 — DC23/
     eng/20220112
LC record available at https://lccn.loc.gov/2021054586

First, I have shown above that there are many seeds of things which support our life, and on the other hand there must be many flying about which make for disease and death. When these by chance or accident have gathered together, and thrown the heavens into turmoil, the air becomes diseased. And all these diseases in their power and pestilence either come from without down through the sky, like clouds and mists, or often they gather together and rise from the earth itself.

—Lucretius, *De Rerum Natura*

Not everything that can be counted counts. Not everything that counts can be counted.

—William Bruce Cameron, *Informal Sociology*

Contents

The End of the World

as We Knew It

Like plagues themselves, this book has a strange history. It originated in a curious coincidence. In November of 2019, I had invited a colleague and friend, Michael Loriaux, to present his most recent research in a graduate seminar I teach each fall in Paris. The general topic had to do with the role of alterity in the constitution of identity, and more specifically with the ways in which two French philosophers, Jacques Derrida and Emmanuel Levinas, conceive of this role. Michael entitled his contribution to the seminar "The End of the World as We Know It." This title was not meant by him to sound quite as apocalyptic as it might appear today, even if what it suggested was anything but harmless. For the world he was referring to was that of a European history marked by increasingly deadly and destructive conflicts, culminating in the Second World War. Michael's presentation was devoted to the efforts made in the wake of that conflict to establish institutions that might help to avoid such lethal repetitions. Little did he or I dream that in the space of a few months a very different type of destruction was about to engulf not just Europe but the world, once again causing millions of deaths.

But the pandemic that was to emerge in Wuhan shortly thereafter, in December of 2019, was not the origin of this book. Rather, it developed in response to a far more limited occasion. One of the readings Michael had suggested we prepare for his seminar was a selection from Camus's novel, *The Plague*. This was the only literary text among those that Michael proposed: other readings included selections from Vatican II, the Treaty of Rome, and the French philosopher of "personalism," Emmanuel Mounier. Having dutifully reread Camus's novel, I was all the more surprised when in his presentation Michael never made mention of it. I found this omission was all the more curious, since I had not been able to figure out just how Camus's novel, written in 1941, had found its way onto Michael's list. I am still not entirely sure. But this uncertainty then became a motive for reflecting not just about the novel, but about the relation of storytelling more generally to plagues, which affect the lives not just of individuals but of collectives.

In the case of Camus, the account of an entirely fictional plague afflicting the Algerian city of Oran in the 1940s clearly had much to do with the situation of occupied France during the war. Camus spent most of that period in metropolitan France, where he could observe firsthand the effects of the German occupation. But reading this in 2019, this implicit if unmistakable juxtaposition of the plague with the Nazi occupation struck me as strangely abstract. The force of the novel was tied to scenes of individual suffering, such as the slow death of a child and the helplessness of the physician trying to save him, rather than to anything like the historical experience of occupied France. To be sure, in both cases, individuals in the face of extreme suffering seemed more or less helpless. But this similarity also highlighted the distance that separated the destructiveness of the plague from that of a politically devastating occupation. The latter was far more associated with deliberate actions of perpetrators, whereas the plague demonstrated its power to destroy independently of human intentions and actions, almost like the force of mortality itself.

It was precisely this divergence between a destructiveness that derives directly from human activity and one that is only indirectly related to it, that moved me to reconsider the distinctive historical significance of the plague—a significance that did not need the emergence of Covid-19 to be confirmed. For some time, the proliferation of epidemics in the postwar period, from AIDS to SARS to MERS to Ebola (to mention just a few), had increasingly concerned epidemiologists and captivated the imagination of writers and film-makers. Political decision makers, by contrast, seemed relatively unconcerned with the potential destructiveness of a force that could not be attributed to the intentional acts of a clearly defined "enemy."

Long before the emergence of Covid-19, then, the stage was set for a confrontation with a phenomenon that was both as old as human history itself, while being as contemporary as the most recent eco-nomic and technological developments. In the experience of plagues, individual and collective, historical and actual, intentional and unin-tentional forces converge to reveal how cultures and societies deal with their vulnerability and mortality. In attacking life processes in what appears to be a relatively spontaneous fashion, plagues resemble events that are often classified as "natural." However, unlike catas-trophes such as tsunamis, earthquakes, volcanic eruptions, and astral collisions, the emergence and evolution of plagues respond not just to natural causes but to preexisting social conditions. If their occur-rence has traditionally been described as a "visitation," the relation of plagues to preexisting conditions reveals them to be invited visi-tors, even if the invitation is anything but deliberate, voluntary, or explicit. Plagues are invited by the specific and even singular "preex-isting conditions" of the places they "visit." As the notion of "visita-tion" suggests, plagues are always on the move. The responses they produce must take this mobility into account.

One of the classic responses to plagues is to isolate: to isolate the sick from the healthy, which means to isolate communities and indi-viduals from each other. But this also goes together with its obverse: that of concentrating and confining, not just the sick with the sick, but the sick with those they might contaminate. This gives rise to dramas in which solitude and separation go hand in hand with hos-tility and aggressivity, but also with solidarity and sympathy. Sin-gular living beings are called upon to redefine their relationship to other singular beings, and in so doing to the collectives to which they belong and on which they variously depend. But they also are drawn to rethink their relationship to themselves: their past, present, and their precarious future. Confronted with a more or less direct and often imminent threat to their survival, their sense of themselves and their relation to others — and to alterity more generally, also in the form of death — can no longer be assured by a blind faith in established conventions, which otherwise, in periods felt to be "normal," tend to stabilize the anxieties that a sense of finitude might produce. Counting the increasingly unpredictable number of victims, singular beings can no longer "count" on conventional wisdom or on the inherited markers of stability to survive.

Where previous accounts can no longer be trusted, "re-counting" becomes necessary. As with contested elections, a recount is required, not however in order to confirm or refute the exactitude of the original count. Rather, in the situation that imposes ever greater separation upon singular beings, recounting becomes necessary, but often in a form I propose to call "frictional" rather than merely "fictional." Frictional storytelling demonstrates that separation can be the condition of communication rather than of solipsistic isolation. As with Boccaccio's *brigada*, the storytellers retreat from the immediate threat but do not cut themselves off from it or from its implications: that is, from its preexisting conditions or possible effects. Whereas fiction might tend to impose a more or less univocal meaning on the plague, friction makes no such claim, but only displays how the *telling* includes but also diverges from the *tallying* of plague victims. The community of tellers is separate and limited in time. After ten days, they return to the perils of a Florence still in the grip of the plague. Their recounting does not provide a direct solution or alternative to the plague's fatal power, but it does illuminate the ways in which singular beings commune with one another, before, during, and sometimes after the "visitation" of the plague. Its recounting thus displays not so much the ravages of the plague itself — practically absent from Boccaccio's stories — but rather those of the "preexisting conditions" to which the plague responds.

"Preexisting conditions" is a phrase taken from the American "healthcare industry," which seeks to amortize the past by refusing "coverage" to persons for previously existing illnesses. This effort to separate and capitalize on the past, however, seeks to deny and control the ways in which preexisting conditions contribute to the "visitation" of plagues and pandemics, to their emergence no less than to their effects. The past rubs up against the present and thereby shapes its future, that of plagues as of everything else. The interconnectedness of events and circumstances across time is why the temptation to isolate the plague as a subject or object of investigation must be resisted. This is what attention to its "frictional recounting" seeks to capture: the encounter with a reality that is as physical as it is linguistic, as singular as it is general, as solitary as it is communal. Here, we consider different manifestations of the "plague" within their trajectories of human and environmental conditions, as documented by writers in the Western tradition who explored a population's confrontation with their shared mortality, which proves also to be a testament to their shared lives.

In this encounter, no one is entirely "safe" or detached, not the narrator, the writer, nor the reader. Although Boccaccio's notion of "compassion" cannot by itself serve to provide the basis of a plague-inspired alternative politics, one which might "save" from future pandemics, it can illuminate what Hölderlin, in his remarks on *Oedipus*, calls the task of establishing "good civic order" (*gute bürgerliche Ordnung*) as a proper response to the plague. Just what, however, would make such an order "good" is, of course, the great question that the plague poses both to politics and to poetics. By confronting individuals and societies with their shared mortality, the plague can either encourage individuals to oppose themselves to others as to "enemies" or to acknowledge what they have in common.

The history of plagues, as outlined here, and in particular their frictional recounting, document the ways in which individuals and societies confront their shared destiny, both by affirming and

13

denying their irreducible involvement of one in another, of one in others.

The forms this involvement takes, despite a certain generality, are always singular. They are determined by the specific cultural and religious traditions to which the texts discussed in this book all belong. It is a European and "Western" tradition, which, as I have elsewhere tried to argue, is tied to monotheism through the persistence of what I call "the monotheistic identity paradigm."[1] If the texts discussed in this book begin with a discussion of plagues in the Bible, it is because many of the narratives of plagues in the centuries following tend to invoke the idea of a divine or transcendent punishment as a way of making sense of pandemics, and ultimately also of the mortality of living beings. But the communicative nature of recounting — whether as storytelling, theater, or essay — strives to establish connections across the distance separating reader from writer, listener from speaker. The stories, plays, and essays inspired by plagues respond to events whose destructiveness seems to defy adequate representation and even understanding, and yet at the same time to demand both. The fact that plague narratives span not just centuries but millennia, provides material for reflection on just how much has changed since their earliest appearance, but also just how much has persisted. If this persistence is the sign of a large-scale but nevertheless limited culture — that informed by monotheism — it should not be too quickly universalized as essentially "human" or "natural."

In insisting on the frictional nature of plague narratives, dramatizations, and essays, I have sought to avoid fictional universalism by foregrounding the singularity of the "preexisting conditions" that frame plague narratives. Such conditions are never absolute, never universal, even if many of their attributes are shared. What may well provide the common denominator against which the distinct singularity of such recounting emerges is the challenge that mortality poses to individuals and their institutions.

Negotiating the complex relationship of the singular and the collective remains one of the most perplexing lessons of the experience the world has been living through, in very unequal measure, since January of 2020. This date marks "the end of the world as we know it," whereby the world we thought we "knew" was perhaps already not so different from the one we are learning to live with. The pandemic has just brought its fractures out into the open.

Freud once suggested that the sign of an effective psychoanalytic interpretation was when the analysand responded by admitting that they "knew it all the time — just had never thought of it."[2] Rereading the recounting of plagues offers the opportunity to rethink what may have been *known* all the time, but not sufficiently *thought*. Such thinking may help to bring about that "good civic order" that could make the end of a world the beginning of another.

CHAPTER ONE

The Local and the General

Repetition, Resonance, Anticipation

The first thing that strikes someone studying the history of "plagues" — a history that seems to be coextensive with the writing of history itself — is how different what came to be known as "the plague" was from the pandemic that emerged in Wuhan, China, at the end of 2019 and that continues today (September 2021). The plague, whose earliest manifestations were recorded over 2,500 years ago, and which devastated much of the world until its cause was identified at the end of the nineteenth century, killed a large percentage of those it afflicted, and it killed them rapidly, within the space of days, not weeks or months. It decimated populations, often over 50% of the localities it "visited," and brought incalculable suffering and disorganization in its wake. Nothing like that can be said of Covid-19. But as epidemiologists warn us, this could have been different. Instead of killing less than 5% of those it afflicts, Covid-19 could have resembled more recent epidemics such as Ebola (Case Fatality Rate 60%), MERS (CFR of 37%), or SARS (CFR 10%).[1] However, in contrast to these far more deadly epidemics, Covid-19, which has a much lower fatality rate, has proved far more contagious and difficult to control because its transmission is spread not just through direct contact but through droplets and much smaller "aerosols," and because it can be spread not just by those who display signs of illness but by those who are either asymptomatic or pre-symptomatic. From the start, asymptomatic and aerosol transmission made it almost impossible to confine to a limited area, especially in this age of global travel and interconnectedness.

But the way in which Covid-19 relates to its environment is significantly different from the plague. This is a consequence of the difference between a bacterial and a viral illness. Bacteria are traditionally defined as microorganisms that are capable of living and reproducing themselves on their own, as it were. As we will see, this definition is not without its problems, since bacteria also require certain environmental supports to exist and reproduce. But they require them in a less internal way than viruses. Indeed, for a long period and even today, one fact has been considered as a reason to disqualify viruses as living beings: viruses are not able to reproduce themselves without invading host organisms and taking over their reproductive mechanisms. That attitude has recently been called into question, since as just mentioned, the reproductive capacity of bacteria is not absolutely self-contained. And thus, the sharp distinction between reproduction that is relatively autonomous, used as a defining characteristic of "life," is no longer considered entirely unproblematic.[2] Nevertheless, it is clear that viruses depend on host organisms, and thus on their environment, in ways that bacteria do not. This also affects their transmissibility, which, as already mentioned in relation to Covid-19, can take place not just through direct physical contact but also through airborne transmission. Moreover, the closer relation between virus and host seems to emphasize the importance of the preexisting condition of the host organism: its receptivity or reactivity, via the immune system, to the intrusions of the virus.

In other words, at least with Covid-19, the susceptibility of persons to infection varies greatly depending both on their individual histories and their living conditions. And the outcome of the infection is also determined by the quality of medical care, even in the absence of a direct treatment or cure. The same factors that made the pandemic inevitable, namely, the degree of worldwide connectedness in an age of globalization, have also influenced the progress of research and treatment of the disease, enabling a communication — but also a competition — that previously was unthinkable. The result is that a vaccine could be produced less than a year after the genome of the virus was made known, whereas previously this would have taken several years. Also, modes of treatment have been developed that, without constituting a cure, have significantly lowered the mortality rate since the disease first emerged.

Despite the differences between a bacterial-caused pandemic — the "plague" in the traditional sense — and the current virus-based pandemic, certain underlying continuities between traditional plagues and the current pandemic remain. Whether viral or bacterial, the spread and seriousness of pandemics, as with all illnesses, depend on what has been labeled "preexisting conditions." This term is itself emblematic of what it names. Although it can and probably should have the general meaning of signifying a current situation that is the result of accumulated factors — in short, of signifying the dependence of the present on the past — in this specific context it reflects a practice of the American "healthcare industry," which has turned healthcare into a profitable commodity. As a result, the dependence of the present on the past is recognized primarily as a means of calculating the best way of maximizing future profits. "Preexisting conditions" thus becomes a means of excluding accumulated risks to this end, by only insuring persons for illnesses they do not already have or are not liable to get. The plague reveals that from a health point of view, as distinct from a profit point of view, the exclusion of "preexisting conditions" is untenable, since these "conditions" also condition the susceptibility to the pandemic, as to any other illness. The plague, however, reveals this on a massive, collective scale, since the preexisting conditions affect not just individuals but specific groups. Here, as elsewhere, Covid-19, like the plagues that preceded it, has a revelatory function: it reveals precisely the existence of "preexisting conditions" that differentiate susceptibility and vulnerability to illness. Everyone is mortal, but not everyone is equally mortal. Or rather, not everyone is mortal in the same way. Thus, it is not just an accident that the advent of Covid-19 has served as a catalyst to stimulate protest movements against preexisting conditions of social and economic inequality. The social classes that benefit from such inequalities also react in much the same way they have always reacted: by deflecting attention from preexisting inequalities toward the victims of those conditions, who are held responsible for the pandemic. During the fourteenth century, as Europe was ravaged by the Black Death (the bubonic plague), Jews were often accused of poisoning the wells and a series of pogroms took place in Germany, Spain, and Northern Europe. The desire to find a culprit — a human cause — for the suffering and death inflicted by pandemics remains active today.

The search for a cause that can then be controlled, if not eradicated, as in the case of scapegoating, can be seen to be a response to the shock effect of plagues. Traditionally, and today as well, the "plague" was experienced and portrayed very much in line with the etymological history of the word in English, French, Latin, Greek, and Hebrew: namely, as a "blow" that strikes suddenly, lethally, and from without.[3] From the point of view of "Western" countries and cultures, plagues are generally said to originate in the "East" just as the forty-fifth President of the United States referred persistently to Covid-19 as "the Chinese virus" — although there is growing evidence that its emergence in Wuhan may not coincide with its origin. Similarly, recent research suggests that the bubonic plague may not have come from the East at all, but may well have been incubated in Northern Europe long before it appeared in Asia.[4] A particularly telling instance of how such scapegoating can function even at the level of what looks like dispassionate scientific discourse is the so-called Spanish flu, "which infected 500 million people — about a third of the world's population at the time — in four successive waves" lasting from February 1918 to April 1920. "The death toll is typically estimated to have been somewhere between 17 . . . and 50 million, making it one of the deadliest pandemics in human history." But despite its name, "the first observations of illness and mortality were documented in the United States, France, Germany and the United Kingdom." How did it come to be called "the Spanish flu"? The explanation is edifying and all too indicative of the political dimension of all plagues, which affect not just individuals but collectives:

> "Spanish flu" is actually a misnomer. The pandemic broke out near the end of World War I, when wartime censors suppressed bad news in the belligerent countries to maintain morale, but newspapers freely reported the outbreak in neutral Spain. These stories created a false impression of Spain as the epicenter, so press outside Spain adopted the name "Spanish" flu. ("Spanish Flu," Wikipedia, https://en.wikipedia.org/wiki/Spanish_flu)

Although the origin of this pandemic has never been definitively identified, the name has remained, providing no doubt both a distraction from its probable US origin and from its ties to the war (it was spread by American soldiers going to Europe). Moreover, to name a pandemic by tying it to a locality is in a sense already to "contain" it lexicographically if not physically, and also to assign "blame" and "guilt" to the country of its putative (if false) origin.

The desire to retrace pandemics to their ultimate origin is thus symptomatic not just of the justifiable medical desire to identify the emergence and possible causes of the disease. It also demonstrates the desire to "contain" a phenomenon by distracting from its connection to a more general political and economic system, which, in the case of the 1918 flu pandemic involved the struggle of competing imperial systems and the interests driving them that produced the First World War. Militarization of conflicts works through the attempt to localize opposing forces in order to destroy them. Pandemics work against such localization, while thriving on the concentration of forces that all militarization produces.

We will have the opportunity to discuss the relation between the plague and war later, in reading Thucydides's account of the plague that afflicted Athens and influenced the course of the Peloponnesian War. For now, however, we should note that the desire to control and eliminate plagues by identifying their origins tends to deny their essentially relational dimension, which in principle cannot be reduced to a single cause or place. Even if Covid-19 first emerged in Wuhan through the passage of the virus from bats to humans (via the intermediary of the pangolin), this would still not suffice to constitute the ultimate cause of the pandemic, which as many epidemiologists have argued, would have to be related to the ecological and social changes in reducing the areas in which non-human life can exist, thus increasing the likelihood of zoonosis, that is, pathogens jumping from non-human to human organisms.[5]

The desire to retrace a dangerous event or phenomenon to a single originating cause that could then be controlled and made into an object of blame, or even of reparations, is also manifest in the suspicion advanced by the Trump administration that the new Coronavirus could have originated in a Wuhan laboratory engaged in biological research. For much of the media and its consumers, the fact that Trump advocates something — hydroxychloroquine, for instance — is sufficient for it to be relegated to the realm of "fake news" and political posturing, and the same holds for his and Mike Pompeo's assertions about the probable laboratory origin of Covid-19. Such rapid dismissals of arguments that far more eminent scientists have found worthy of consideration — I am thinking here of Nobel Prize winner and co-discoverer of the HIV virus, Professor Luc Montagnier — is indicative not just of the shrinking of the field of public discussion and its reduction to polemics, but even more of the underlying insistence on certainty and the growing incapacity to accept uncertainty as a condition of dialogue. This too must be counted as a "preexisting condition" that powerfully shapes the responses to and experiences of plagues and pandemics.[6] Obviously, this is not a controversy that a non-specialist can begin to evaluate fully; but what does seem to emerge is the overhasty tendency to dismiss arguments that do not easily conform to certain expectations or interests, however complex and contradictory those expectations and interests may be.

The idea that the pandemic could have derived from a laboratory mistake is particularly revealing of these contradictions. On the one hand, it presupposes that the origin of the catastrophe involves a large-scale institutional effort, not just of the Chinese government since the Wuhan laboratory was supported by many international agencies. In one way, this can be reassuring, for instance, as opposed to the more ecological theory. But it is also disconcerting, since the arguments being made by Montagnier, Perez, and Tritto indicate how ill-equipped human society is to control the consequences of its acts and intentions. Putting aside for the moment the fact that one of the supporting studies has been retracted, the arguments made by Montagnier, Perez, and Tritto in favor of a possible laboratory accident as the origin of the virus do not imply that it was intentionally produced as a possible biochemical weapon — an activity that is pursued worldwide by almost all the "major" world powers, despite almost all having signed on to the 1972 Biological Weapons Convention prohibiting the development of such weapons. Rather, what the Montagnier-Perez-Tritto interpretations suggest is that humans risk losing control over their products — a fear that has haunted societies for most of the modern period, which has seen the explosion of technological advances but also their increasing use for military purposes, that is, for destruction and conquest.

This specter both stimulates and discredits what might be called "causal" thinking, and the recent pandemic has both accentuated its loss of authority and the desire to preserve it at any cost. Causal thinking seeks to establish firm links between temporal events in order to exercise a measure of control over the future. But such links presuppose that the events identified as causes can be more or less clearly delineated and defined. The history of the plague provides ample evidence for the effectiveness of such approaches, but also evidence of its limitations. The ravages of the plague, in its bubonic and pneumonic forms, were effectively controlled, if not eliminated, following the identification of the bacillus that causes the illness in 1894 by the Swiss-French physician, Alexandre Yersin. His name has since been attached to the bacillus, although it was more or less simultaneously discovered by a Japanese bacteriologist, Kitasato Shibasaburō, who has been largely forgotten. This discovery, together with the development of antibiotics, brought the plague largely under control, although it did not eliminate it: there continue to be isolated outbreaks up until the present (one of which shortly preceded the emergence of Covid-19).

But in the case of illnesses caused by viruses, identification of the causative agent seems to be less propitious to controlling the disease, and this may well have to do with the way viruses interact with host organisms not just to replicate but also to mutate. Such mutations are the main reason why the search for a vaccine against the HIV virus has been unsuccessful and is considered extremely unlikely to succeed. The same capacity to mutate is also the reason why the immunity conferred by the vaccine against the seasonal flu is short-lived and must be renewed each year.

In short, by comparison with bacteria, viruses are much more of a moving target. And in the case of Covid-19, this mobility also affects their targets within the body. They can attack not just the respiratory system, but many other parts of the organism as well: the heart, the circulatory system, and even the brain. Finally, the destructive effects produced seem to survive the disappearance of the virus itself, producing symptoms long after the person has tested negative for the virus and is deemed to have "recovered."

But as already mentioned, movement is only part of the way in which viruses, and plagues more generally, exist. If movement is defined in the traditional "locomotive" sense, as going from one fixed point to another, the capacity of plagues and pandemics to spread is conditioned by their environment, including the "preexisting conditions" of the places they infest. The words of Antonin Artaud, in his 1931 lecture, "The Theater and the Plague," echo an insight that resounds throughout the history of plagues: "The *Grand-Saint-Antoine* did not bring the plague to Marseille. It was already there."[7] In what sense the plague was "already there" we will have the opportunity to discuss later on. But without going into details, we find that again and again, the encounter with the plague is described in a dual and contradictory sense. On the one hand, the plague arrives with a violent shock, an outbreak, striking not just individuals but places. In this sense, the progress of its infection can be measured in terms of time and space. It ravages specific localities, not just persons, and the speed with which it does so seems measurable. On the other hand, its outbreak is often experienced as a kind of repetition or recurrence, which makes its spatial and temporal measurement more difficult to determine. Thus, some argue that its mortality rate should be measured in comparison to that of previous, pre-plague years. Other arguments include considering the life-expectancy of its victims as part of the calculation. But the movement of the plague is also difficult to gauge because its position is never unequivocally localizable. As Tarrou, one of the main characters in Camus's novel, *The Plague,* tells his friend, Dr. Rieux, "To make things simpler, Rieux, let me begin by saying [that] I had [the] plague already, long before I came to this town and encountered it here."[8] The shock of the plague as something new is mitigated by the experience of it through a kind of *déjà vu.* This is not the least of its uncanny effects.

In short, if the plague is conditioned by preexisting factors, then its arrival, however abrupt and shocking, is never absolute. Its visitation depends on the "host" who extends it a certain hospitality, however involuntarily. In this sense, the plague is revelatory, but what it reveals is an unsettled relation of the present to the past, and this inevitably emphasizes the uncertainty of the future. It is perhaps this uncertainty that causes many reports of the plague to take the form of retrospective narratives, whether as stories, histories, or a mixture of both. Later on, I will try to characterize these narratives neither as fictional, in the sense of purely imaginary or invented, nor as accurate histories, but as *frictional.* Frictional narratives are both historical and fictional, repetitive and made-up. But this made-up fictional aspect is never absolute, for it involves the way in which the present resonates with the past in anticipating the future. It is this strange mixture of revelation, resonance, and anticipation that tends to comprise every plague, including the coronavirus, which was initially described as being totally "novel" but in the meanwhile seems to have become uncannily familiar. It is this uncanny novelty that calls for a *recounting*.

The Tell-Tale Story (Walter Benjamin)

Many of the documents that transmit previous experiences of plagues take the form of stories. From the Bible, to Thucydides, to Boccaccio, and beyond, the encounter with the plague is documented in narratives. To understand not "the plague" or "pandemics" in general, but the ways they are experienced, therefore, requires at the outset some reflection on storytelling more generally. Why do people tell stories, and what might this tell us about their — and our — experience of plagues?

In 1936, Walter Benjamin published an essay, whose title has been translated as "The Storyteller," that sought to address these questions, albeit in a more negative mode. Benjamin began by noting that the art of storytelling seemed to be disappearing, in part because of what today might be called "post-traumatic stress disorder." People returning from the horrors of the First World War were "not richer but poorer in communicable experience."[9] Although most dramatically manifested by the effects of the war, this loss of communicable experience was, Benjamin argued, part of a much more general process in which the oral transmission of experiences was increasingly marginalized through technological, socio-economic, and media-historical developments.

Benjamin's text is curious for a number of reasons. At the time he wrote it, he was increasingly dependent on his writings to finance his life in exile, and this essay was written in response to a commission from a periodical. It was written about a writer who was and probably still is considered to have a minor role in Russian nineteenth-century literature: Nikolai Leskov. And it was written concerning a writer that Benjamin could not read in the original — one of the very few instances where he devoted a major text to someone he could read only in translation. But, above all, it was written about a writer at the same time that the arguments Benjamin seems to be developing concern the oral medium of storytelling. I will return to this shortly. Perhaps it is one reason why Benjamin, a recent biography claims, "attached no particular importance" to this essay.[10] Nevertheless, despite or perhaps because of the problems just mentioned, the essay outlines a theory of narration that is uniquely illuminating for the texts we are going to be considering in this book.

But before proceeding any further, it is important to note that the English translation of the title as "The Storyteller" is not quite accurate. Benjamin's title is shorter, simpler, but also more general: "Der Erzähler," literally, "The Teller." Something like a "story" may be implied in the German word, but this implication is not absolutely necessary: the emphasis is on the "telling," not on the "story." As we will see shortly, this distinction is not insignificant.

Telling, according to Benjamin, proceeds "from mouth to mouth," a phrase he repeats several times in the first sections of his essay. But here as elsewhere, reading Benjamin requires one to go beyond the individual statements and declarations and to reflect on their relation to other elements of the text. Despite what looks like an emphasis on oral storytelling, the teller that Benjamin is writing about, Nikolai Leskov as mentioned, was a writer, not an oral storyteller. His stories may be related to this tradition, but they remain written texts. Very soon in his essay, it appears that what Benjamin is concerned with is not so much the oral quality of narration, but its corporeal dimension: he will go on to relate the storyteller to handwork, to the hand, and thus to the singular body. It is not so much the mouth or even the voice per se that concern Benjamin as it is the role of the body and everything it involves in the process.

But we are getting ahead of ourselves. Let us return to the way Benjamin introduces his subject, which for him means, above all, defining his relationship to it:

> Familiar though his name may be to us, the storyteller in his vital effectiveness (*Wirksamkeit*) is by no means fully present. He is already remote from us and . . . is becoming ever more distant. To present someone like Leskov as a storyteller does not mean bringing him closer to us but rather increasing our

separation from him.... This separation ... [is] dictated to us by an experience that is available to us almost daily. It tells us (*sie sagt uns*) that the art of
storytelling is coming to an end. (I; translation modified)

There are many reasons that Benjamin gives in this essay to explain
the end of the art of storytelling: the traumatic and, above all,
mechanical violence done to the human body in war; the rise of
information that seeks to explain everything definitively and leave
nothing open; the rise of the novel that seeks to present the reader
with a complete and meaningful life and thereby once again to close
off its possible significance. But as with the roughly contemporaneous and far more famous essay on "The Work of Art in the Age of its
Technical Reproducibility," here, too, the contrast between the old
and the new — between the oral and the written tradition — is less
clear-cut than Benjamin often seems to suggest. And this because,
in a strange sense, it is storytelling that is closer to the "reproducibility" manifested by the media technologies of his time — film and
photography, but also phonographs — than the more recent forms of
the novel or of the Information Age. The latter insists on the immediate and full intelligibility of the news, today emphasized by the
cliché "breaking": the new may break with the old but only in order
to demonstrate its self-identity and meaningfulness. The novel, for
its part, seeks to compensate for the isolation of its readers by drawing a conclusive and definitive trait at the end of a life. The story, by
contrast, is never complete; it is always episodic, part of a discontinu-
ous sequence from which it separates itself but never fully breaks.
The storyteller is also not an "author" in the modern sense, since
s/he is always a re-teller of tales that preexist and that are transformed in their repetition. In this sense, the story is essentially
repeatable. Both its inception and its reception reflect and pro-
long this process. In German, Benjamin describes its reception as
"*Lauschen*," as a "listening," which is a far more involving and far less
cognitive activity than is "hearing." One listens to a story, one does
not simply "hear" it. Listening is a reproductive and transformative

process, which is therefore linked to the special kind of memory that distinguishes the story from the epic, the novel, as well as from the news media. In section XIII, Benjamin distinguishes "the eternalizing memory of the novelist" (in German, *Gedächtnis*), from the "short-lived one of the teller," which he calls in German, curiously, *Eingedenken*:

> The former is consecrated to the *one* hero, the *one* wandering, or the *one* battle; the second to the *many* dispersed occurrences (XIII).

The German word *Eingedenken* is curious here because normally it designates the opposite of what Benjamin has it signify: it is closer to the English "commemorate" than to simply memory or remembrance. And yet that would imply that it is dedicated precisely to "the one" rather than to the "many." The distinction Benjamin is trying to articulate here can be clarified, perhaps, if one notices that the prefix of the word he is using — *Ein* (*gedenken*) — is ambiguous, signifying both "one" and "into." In the case of the epic *Gedächtnis*, "one" stands for unity and individuality — of the hero as of his adventures and accomplishments — in the most literal sense, which is to say, indivisibility. In the case of the story, by contrast, the "one" in German changes from an independent word to a prefix, modifying a thought process of remembrance: *Ein-gedenken*. One could also think of this word as "commemoration." The point being that the *ein-* changes from something designating individuality and unity to something designating a singularity that is not identical with itself since it requires memory to exist, and yet in being remembered, it is no longer itself, no longer unique. This is why here and elsewhere such singularity is both unique and plural *at the same time*, even if the *sameness* of that time retains a certain heterogeneity and openness.

This also applies to the opening lines of the essay; in the first published translation, words used by Benjamin in German, *lebendige Wirksamkeit*, were translated as "living immediacy." This has been corrected in the more recent Harvard edition to read "living efficacy." In my attempt to render it, I opted for "effectiveness." Still, the latter two are too teleological, suggesting the accomplishment of a goal rather than the production of effects. There is nothing "immediate" about *Wirksamkeit* but also little that suggests "efficiency" in any form. *Wirksamkeit* involves simply the effects that something can produce, its "working," and as such implies a certain separation from its present state. This is why Benjamin begins his essay by accentuating and reflecting on our distance from the storyteller; such an awareness, he argues, is indispensable if one is to "present" his "figure," literally, "place it before us" (in German, *darstellen*: "place there"). Benjamin's storyteller will thus be placed in front of us and yet also distant from us: in German, this is the important difference between *vorstellen* and *darstellen*: the *dar*, "there," is neither here nor there in the sense of being essentially related to our position. German distinguishes between two sorts of "there": *dort*, the opposite of here, and *da*, which is not the opposite of anything, but is simply "there" where we are not.

Although Benjamin's "story" here suggests a linear decline or loss of experience, as in his roughly contemporaneous essay on reproducibility, he also warns against understanding the crisis of storytelling as a linear process of decline:

> Nothing would be more fatuous than to want to see in it merely a "symptom of decay," let alone a "modern" symptom. It is, rather, a concomitant symptom of the secular productive forces of history (IV).

What Benjamin seems to be suggesting is that "the secular productive forces of history" accentuate and accompany, but do not simply cause, the reduction of plurality to unity, of dispersion to concentration, that finds its literary culmination in the novel and its medial culmination in the new media (which Benjamin refers to as "information"), but that can be traced back to emphasis of the ancient epic on the single hero, the single event, the single conquest (XIII).

In short, the storyteller appeals to a memory that is both singular and plural, unique and dispersed, separate and yet connected. This is also why, in the second section of his essay, Benjamin can identify two figures as constitutive of the storyteller: the seaman, who wanders out into the world, and the landman, who stays at home to cultivate the land and its traditions. But once again this duality should not be construed as a mutually exclusive opposition, since only their "most intimate interpenetration" can allow the story to realize its fullest potential: "In it was combined the lore of faraway places ... with the lore of the past as it best reveals itself to natives of a place" (II). In short, the story articulates the relation between the local and the general, between what is near and what is distant. In this respect, it has its own aura, which Benjamin famously defined as the appearance of a certain distance in what seems to be near.

But all of these determinations and definitions pale before what I take to be the most significant dimension of Benjamin's theory of storytelling: the fact that it is first and foremost a *response*, and a response that seeks to evoke further responses. To what does it respond? Above all, to a certain disorientation, my best attempt to render in English the word that Benjamin uses, which is *Ratlosigkeit* (V). This word, based on the root word, *Rat*, is almost impossible to render in idiomatic English. It names a situation of perplexity, in which there is a need or demand for advice, or, as it is translated in the published English versions, for "counsel." I prefer the word "advice" although the German word used by Benjamin encompasses both advice and counsel. The word *Rat* in German has a much wider range of uses than either of the two English words taken separately. As a verb, *raten*, it implies the notion of conjecture, guessing, divining, with the more everyday and practical idea of "advising." If the "art of storytelling" is dying out, according to Benjamin — a dramatic assertion that as we have begun to see requires infinite qualification — then it is because the need and demand for advice is diminishing, under the influence, above all, of "information" and related discourses. These discourses provide "answers" that preclude the demand for further responses. Every answer is a response, but not every response is an answer. Responses without definitive answers are what distinguish the story, according to Benjamin, from both the novel and the news media, just as it distinguishes the medieval "chronicler" from the modern "historian." The latter explains, whereas the ancient chronicler or historian, such as Herodotus, recounts without providing a definitive conclusion, thus leaving it up to the listener or reader to decide, which is to say, to respond in turn.

In other words, the story cannot be understood as constituting a self-contained totality, literally meaning-ful. Instead, it provides counsel:

> In every case the storyteller is someone who has counsel for his readers. . . . Counsel is less an answer to a question than a proposal concerning the continuation of a story that is just unfolding. To seek this counsel, one would first have to be able to tell the story (IV).

To seek counsel presupposes that "one would first have to be able to tell the story" — but to tell the story in a way that puts it in the present participle, as something ongoing but never complete, as something "that is just unfolding." In other words, to tell a story means to acknowledge that the telling is caught up in the story as incomplete and ongoing, and therefore can never attain a full overview of its trajectory. Every story is of limited duration, like a limited, mortal life: it cannot hope to go on forever. But it can hope to defer the end and to give rise to new and other stories. As with Scheherazade, whom, according to Benjamin, "thinks of a fresh story whenever her tale comes to a stop" (XIII), every storyteller struggles not to overcome death but to delay its execution by providing a new story. What survives is not the individual story nor the individual storyteller, but the process of telling.

The following textual example given by Benjamin is in this respect very telling; it is drawn from a story told, or retold (because the event recounted existed previously in other stories), by the German writer, Johann Peter Hebel, called "Unhoped-for Reunion" (*Unverhofftes Wiedersehen*). The narrative recounts the story of a young miner who on the eve of his wedding is killed in an accident at the bottom of a mine shaft. Decades later, a body is excavated from the abandoned tunnel, and his former bride to be, now grown old, recognizes her fiancé in the corpse that has been preserved by being saturated with iron vitriol. This is how Hebel describes the many years between the death of the miner and the rediscovery of his body:

> In the meantime, the city of Lisbon was destroyed by an earthquake, and the Seven Years War came and went, and Emperor Francis I died, and the Jesuit Order was abolished, and Poland was partitioned, and Empress Maria Theresa died, and Struensee was executed. America became independent, and the united French and Spanish forces were unable to capture Gibraltar. The Turks locked up General Stein in the Veteraner Cave in Hungary, and Emperor Joseph died. King Gustavus of Sweden conquered Russian Finland, and the French Revolution and the long war began, and Emperor Leopold II went to his grave. Napoleon captured Prussia, and the English bombarded Copenhagen, and the peasants sowed and harvested. The millers ground, the smiths hammered, and the miners dug for veins of ore in their underground workshops. But when in 1809 the miners at Falun . . . (XI).

Benjamin gives only a short gloss:

> Never has a storyteller embedded his report deeper in natural history than Hebel manages to do in this chronology. Read it carefully. Death appears in it with the same regularity as that of the Reaper in the processions that pass round the cathedral clock [Strasbourg] at noon (XI).

Let us for a moment dwell on this passage and read it carefully, as Benjamin suggests. Note the repetition of death. In general, those who die are all sovereigns: Emperor Francis I, Empress Maria Theresa, Emperor Joseph, Emperor Leopold II — the one exception being Struensee, a German physician who became the lover of the Danish Queen, Caroline-Mathilde and who was ultimately executed; the death of the poor miner is thus put in parallel with the death of ruling figures. The relation of the story to time is thus marked by the mortality of individual living beings, whether great and powerful or not. The story, in contrast to certain religions, has no "answer" for this, but it nevertheless responds to it, in part by including a certain discontinuity and finitude in its own structure of repetition.

The story is, as Benjamin asserts, coming to an end. But in a certain sense, it has always been both coming to an end and deferring its end through the production of new stories. Although such stories constitute "a chain of tradition" in which "one links to the next," that link also underscores the gaps that the links bridge but do not eliminate. On both ends of the chain or the more multidirectional "web" (XIII), there are repetitions and a very unusual kind of reproducibility:

> Storytelling is always the art of repeating stories, and this art is lost when the stories are no longer retained. It is lost because there is no more weaving and spinning to go on while they are being listened to. The more self-forgetful the listener is, the more deeply is what he listens to impressed upon his memory. When the rhythm of work has seized him, he listens to the tales in such a way that the gift of retelling them comes to him all by itself. This then is the nature of the web in which the gift of storytelling is cradled. (VIII)

The repeating of stories is unusual because, Benjamin insists, it goes together not with the prolongation of a self-identical subject, the author, but with a certain self-forgetting, of the listener. In listening to the story, listeners learn to forget their selves, or at least a certain aspect of their histories. This allows what Benjamin calls "the rhythm of work" to take over, and this allows "the retelling" of them to "come to him" as a "gift." Storytelling is a gift because it is never the property or product of the teller alone.

This passage is a good example of how what Benjamin is describing as "listening" and "telling" converge with a certain form of reading and writing and also, how this convergence demarcates itself from how they might traditionally be construed. When Benjamin calls storytelling an "art" and when he describes its reception as governed by a "rhythm of work" that in turn engenders — "cradles" — "the gift of storytelling," he is using the words "art" and "work" in a very different way from how they are traditionally conceived; for both words are usually understood as the product of highly self-conscious intentional activity: artists, like workers, are supposed to know what their goal is, what they are trying to produce. This, as Marx remarks in commenting on Aristotle, is what distinguishes the purposive activity of insects or other animals from human art or work.[11] Humans know what they are producing; bees do not. But the work Benjamin is alluding to here is not work as a self-conscious process, which is probably why he introduces the word "rhythm": it describes a recurrent pattern but not necessarily one that is self-conscious or self-reflexive. Such rhythms mimic the production of identity through their recurrence while at the same time undermining it and allowing the emergence of a certain "self-forgetfulness," which is nothing more than a sensitivity to impulses that is no longer governed by constraints of identification. This involves "listening" not only to what comes from without but to what usually is denied from within and which therefore constitutes an internal exterior. Affirming our distance from Leskov, and from storytellers in general, involves both acknowledging the power of social constraints to self-identify, and at the same time accepting their limitations. It involves what Nietzsche once called an "active forgetting"[12] and is akin to the receptivity that Freud asked his patients to strive for: that is, he asked them to try to suspend all conscious expectations as much as possible in order to "freely associate," which is to say, to allow memories, thoughts, and responses that were otherwise inaccessible to become conscious. Translated onto the situation of listening to stories, this suggests an attitude that is neither active, in the sense of mobilizing self-conscious concepts and expectations, nor passive, in the sense of simply reacting to what comes from outside. Rather, *responding* here involves precisely allowing certain impulses — verbal, gestural, etc. — to resonate with previous experiences without demanding that they form a meaningful and unified whole and thereby be assimilated into a sense of oneself as a continuum.

The alternative to this constraining sense of self is a heightened sensitivity to one's surroundings and to one's past — to preexisting conditions and circumstances:

> Storytelling . . . does not aim to convey the pure essence of the thing, like information or a report. It sinks the thing into the life of the storyteller, in

order to bring it out of him again.... Storytellers tend to begin their story
with a presentation of the circumstances in which they themselves have
learned what is to follow (IX).

To "sink the thing into the life of the storyteller" describes the point
of departure of the story: its initiating framework is "the life" of a
singular, living being. But this singular living being is not isolated
as is the individual in many nineteenth-century novels; life in the
singular is indissolubly bound up with its environment, with the
lives of others, and with others who are not necessarily alive. This
is particularly the case with Boccaccio, who (as we will see) begins
the *Decameron* with a long description of the hideous ravages of the
plague in Florence, and who insists that this brutal introduction is
absolutely necessary in order to appreciate the beauty of the stories
that follow. The tension between the fate of singular living beings
and their more general environment — which is not just spatial but
also temporal — is one of the traits that distinguishes the plague from
other catastrophic events. For the plague is both individual and collective: it strikes individuals with deadly force, but it strikes them
as members of a collective: of a city, a town, an army, a religion, a
region. The plague in this sense is both local and general. The stories
it generates must take this into account. As we will see, they will do
this in part by trying to count the devastating effects of the plague,
and then by recounting those effects insofar as they escape mere
enumeration. This counting and recounting also characterizes the
position of the storyteller, who, as Benjamin puts it (at the beginning of XI) in one of his most memorable, and enigmatic, phrases,
"has borrowed his authority from death." Because the plague is both
local and collective, singular and general, it confronts the limitation
of individual living beings with the fate of the group to which they
belong but also from which they are always more or less separated. It
never strikes individuals in isolation, which is why individuals try to
isolate themselves to escape its ravages. But such attempts can never
be entirely successful, because the plague reveals how intertwined

individuals are and must be with others. Nevertheless, it still strikes individuals in their singularity, which means in their bodily existence. And the bodies of individuals can never simply be absorbed into or transcended by the "body politic," the social or religious "body" to which they belong. Benjamin tries to emphasize how this corporeal aspect is both intrinsic to storytelling — it is the corporeal, not the oral, that defines its one pole — but how it at the same time is inevitably distanced through the process of telling, which transforms the body into a signifying agent, in language and in gesture. "The figure of the storyteller," Benjamin writes, "gets its full corporeality only for someone who can picture" it both as seaman and as cultivator, tied to the ocean and to the earth, to the near as to the distant. But when the plague comes to "visit," the foreign invades the home, and the two can no longer be easily separated.

Although Benjamin does not mention it, the great Western epic of homecoming, the *Odyssey*, suggests that something similar may apply to life in general, and that the plague only intensifies this indwelling of the foreign in the domestic. The *Odyssey* does not end with the return of Odysseus; it continues beyond the return (*nostos*) through the prophesy of Tiresias, whom Odysseus has encountered on his trip to the land of the dead to see his mother. Tiresias, who alone among the dead seems to have retained his powers, tells him that after returning home and reclaiming his property, he will once again have to leave it and go to foreign lands where the oars he carries on his shoulders will be mistaken for plowshares by those who know nothing of the sea. Only then, in this remote country — according to Tiresias — will Odysseus be able to make proper sacrifices to his arch divine enemy, Poseidon, and thus acquire the possibility of a calm and peaceful end of life. But even then, the *Odyssey* does not come to rest, since its final book describes the danger of civil war — which in Thucydides will turn out to be a close relative of the plague — as the family members of the suitors killed by Odysseus threaten to make war against him. The epic thus does not so much end as it falls apart inconclusively, which is perhaps why this non-ending is so little remembered and discussed, and why, like stories, it can give rise to further storytelling.

In short, even the most epic of epics, the *Odyssey*, tends to confirm Benjamin's insight that "there is no story for which the question, 'What comes next?' could not be asked" (XIV).

If the storyteller has only "borrowed" his authority from death, it is because "death" has no authority that it could *give* to anyone, apart from the gift of telling. If death can be imagined as having any authority, it can only be as a result of a Being who has created it along with life and who regards it as his property and prerogative. It is to this Being and to a few of the stories in which his legacy has been transmitted that we will turn next.

CHAPTER TWO

Monotheological Antecedents:

Life against the Living

(Genesis, Exodus)

As we have seen, Walter Benjamin's account of narrating — which itself is a kind of narrative describing the decline of the art of storytelling as concomitant with the rise of "information" and the novel — describes storytelling as a response to a demand for "advice" or "counsel": *Rat*. At the same time that he portrays it according to a familiar and indeed theologically based pattern of loss, the loss of experience, he also tries to modify this more or less linear and culturally conservative model by reminding his readers that "nothing would be more foolish" than to conceive "the end of the art of storytelling" as a "manifestation of decadence" (*Verfallserscheinung*), much less a (distinctively) "modern" one. Rather, he suggests, rather lamely, that "perhaps it is only a concomitant manifestation of secular historical productive forces, which have gradually removed narration (*Erzählung*) from the realm of living speech while allowing a new beauty to be sensed in its disappearance" (IV).

The demand for "advice," for guidance, for a knowledge that is not sure and certain but perhaps probable and practical, is indeed "concomitant" insofar as it articulates both a transhistorical and a historical preexisting condition. The transhistorical condition has to do with the difficulty that beings have to conceive of the world without them;[1] and the historical condition has to do with the fact that the conundrum of mortality is experienced only and always as a way of being in the world, a world that is decisively structured by those "secular . . . productive forces" to which Benjamin refers, and to the social organization to which they give rise. The result is an increasingly undermined sense of individual solitude (*Einsamkeit*) as the basis of communal experience that leads to a sense of "profound disorientation" (*Ratloskeit*) not just of humans in general or of social classes in particular but of what Benjamin designates as "the living" (*des Lebenden*, IV). The experience of mortality becomes particularly acute in such a situation. However, this experience is not limited to that historical configuration. And the separation and distancing that Benjamin tends to associate with the modern period and to some extent with more recent technological developments also applies to language more generally, which, as Jacques Derrida has persuasively argued, can never attain the kind of immediacy or presence that is often associated with the spoken word.

This does not mean that the desire for such presence does not exist and persist. And indeed, insofar as the conundrum of mortality drives the desire for *Rat,* and hence for storytelling, it is instructive to go back to one of the most influential stories for a large segment of the world, and not just in its "Western" part. I am thinking here of the first books of the Hebrew Bible, which describe not just the creation of the world and of life, but the radical break between a life that would be eternal and a life that is limited and finite. Inasmuch as all aspects of plagues demonstrate the violence to which living beings are susceptible as mortals, it is important to reflect on just how the emergence of mortality is described in this "story."

As the result of a universal and exclusive Creator God, life initially is described without any relation to death. In the King James Version, there is a phrase that occurs seventeen times in the account of the creation, beginning with the emergence of living beings, first plants, and then animal life. It is the phrase "after his kind":

> And God said, Let the earth bring forth grass, the herb yielding seed, and the fruit tree yielding fruit after his kind, whose seed is in itself, upon the earth: and it was so (Gen. 1:11).

The fact that all living creatures, beginning with grass, are designated as created "after his kind," reflects the universal nature of the Creator; but it also suggests that the mode of life is both eternal and self-sustaining: the earth brings forth grass, the seed yields the herb, the fruit tree yields fruit — all "after his kind": universal and self-contained, "whose seed is in itself, upon the earth." Just as the Creator God is universal and self-contained, so too the living creatures that he engenders. Life at this point is self-sustaining and without end, contained in a continuous circularity of the generic "kind"; later on, Hegel, at the end of his *Philosophy of Nature*, will make the same point about "nature" in arguing that in nature, the individual perishes but the species remains — an argument that for him demonstrates the essentially spiritual (*geistig*) nature of "nature." It is tied to its universality, which in its earliest founding story is a reflection of the universality of the Being from which it stems.

The problem, however, is that it is precisely this reflection and the continuity it suggests that causes the story to continue and in a certain sense to undo its initial state. Human beings are said to be created in the image of their creator. But when they seek to interpret that relationship as one of continuity, if not equality, they are irrevocably distanced from their goal. God makes this clear when he commands Adam to "freely eat" of "every tree in the garden" except "the tree of the knowledge of good and evil; thou shalt not eat of it: for in the day that thou eatest thereof thou shall surely die" (Gen. 2:16–17). Up to this point, created life on earth has been admonished by the Creator to "be fruitful and multiply" (1:22) without limitation. Only in face of the tree of the knowledge of good and evil — which is to say, only in the face of a knowledge that transcends the creation up to that point, since in it there is only "good" and nothing "evil" — only in the face of this "knowledge," which is a certain form of non-knowledge since it has no object, does the story of a life without end stumble and "fall." And it falls out of its own weight, as it were, of its own impulse, which is the impulse to be "like" the Creator, who is eternal, universal, but also — and here is perhaps the rub — singular. The Creator will always demand exclusive adherence and will go on to distinguish himself from all competitors, starting with Adam and Eve themselves. But they seek only to carry to its logical conclusion the fact that they have been created in the image of a Being without end — a life without death. And it is this that will introduce death, not directly, as promised by God, but indirectly as a form of life charged with suffering and scarcity, a life whose limitation does not simply come at its "end" but throughout.

In short, condemnation to a life of suffering, labor, and death is described as the result of the desire precisely to overcome these limitations, and in particular that of mortality. The following words of the Creator leave little doubt about this:

> Behold, the man is become as one of us, to know good and evil and now, lest he put forth his hand and take also of the tree of life, and eat, and live for ever: therefore the Lord God sent him forth from the garden of Eden, to till the ground from whence he was taken (Gen. 3:22–23).

Death, in short, is the result of an intentional act, a transgression, but one that is, as it were, preprogrammed in the nature of the creation itself: man is created in the image and likeness of a being that is immortal. His effort to complete the likeness, to attain an immortality (that in a certain sense already obtains in the garden of Eden) opens the story to innumerable continuations, which continue to mark a great part of their history, including that of those "secular productive forces" to which Benjamin somewhat enigmatically refers in his essay. What is perhaps most important to retain from this reading for our approach to the experience of the plague is that death itself is a punishment for a transgression, and thus acquires a certain meaning qua justification. In some theologies, death marks not just the prolongation of suffering but its intensification, albeit in another world. But with the plague, that world comes home to earth.

In discussing the plague — whether in the singular or in the plural — it is necessary at some point, and preferably earlier rather than later, to examine just wherein the disaster associated with that word differs from other cosmic or worldwide catastrophes, such as the huge asteroid that struck the earth some 66 million years ago known as the Chicxulub impact, which resulted in the sudden mass extinction of three-quarters of the plant and animal species, called the Cretaceous-Paleogene S (K-Pg) extinction event. That such catastrophes continue to haunt the contemporary mind is documented by the existence of "Asteroid Day," celebrated annually in memory of the Siberian Tunguska event that took place on June 30, 1908, and co-founded by none other than Stephen Hawking. Films such as *Armageddon*, Lars von Trier's *Melancholia*, to the recent *Don't Look Up* testify to the continuing force and fascination of this form of catastrophe. Such so-called impact events have in common with the plague the sense of originating from without, and hence, of being able to impact the earth, with more or less catastrophic if not apocalyptic consequences. But despite being often experienced as a more or less sudden blow, the plague, as we have discussed, is not only an external event, but an internal one as well. This characteristic it shares not so much with impact events as with earthquakes, another world-shaking event, whose destructive force, however, does not arise from a collision with an external body but from the explosive force of collisions taking place within the earth. It is easy to see how impact events and earthquakes represent two different images of destruction; the first has to do with trajectories, with the way the earth is moving through space. Hence, in *Armageddon*, the ultimately victorious efforts of Bruce Willis, aided by NASA, to destroy the oncoming asteroid are achieved through an atomic explosion — in other words, to counter a non-human force with a humanly generated one, to preempt the fatal collision with a human controlled one. In the case of earthquakes, it is difficult to imagine such a heroic (and militarized) solution, given that the danger is both internal and structural. The plague shares characteristics with both of these archetypical catastrophes, involving both external circumstances and internal preexisting conditions. And yet it distinguishes itself from them, from natural as well as from cosmic catastrophes, in a way that a return to its Biblical depiction can help to reveal.

If Armageddon refers to the New Testament account of a world-ending struggle between the forces of good and evil — a notion that Protestant fundamentalism has continued to entertain and that in some ways determines its political worldview — then the Biblical accounts of the plague are almost all to be found in the Old Testament, and this not by accident. For the few mentions of plague that occur in the New Testament are mainly there in order to demonstrate the force of Jesus as Healer, as the one who can save the world and in particular mankind from its mortal future.[2]

The first major section in which plagues are described comes in Exodus 7–11, where God uses them as ways of demonstrating his existence to the Egyptian pharaoh, who denies knowing anything about him, and thus to make the pharaoh recognize his power if not his exclusive divinity. Through Moses, God is working to extract the Israelites, "my people," from the condition of slavery they endure in Egypt. To this end, he visits a series of afflictions on pharaonic Egypt, many of which would not today be classified as plagues in the strict sense. But they reveal something about what has been associated with the plague that is essential to its experience. Here are the ten plagues: (1) rivers are turned to blood; (2) frogs overrun the country; (3) lice or gnats infest the area; (4) wild animals or flies do the same; (5) a pestilence is visited upon livestock; (6) boils appear on the bodies of Egyptians; (7) thunderstorms of hail and fire rain down, destroying the land; (8) locusts devastate the harvest, thus depriving the country of its basic food supply; (9) darkness blankets the country for three days; and finally, worst of all, (10) killing of the firstborn of all Egyptian families, thus severely impacting the continuation of traditions and national identity through procreation.

Of these ten events that are described in Exodus, only three correspond to what later will be known as the plague: the pestilence visited upon the livestock, boils, and the death of the firstborn (although the plague was rarely so selective). The others seem quite remote

44

from the plague. And yet I want to suggest that they reflect what distinguishes it precisely from the other global catastrophes mentioned: impact events and earthquakes in particular. For of the other "plagues" visited upon Egypt, almost all affect the indispensable conditions of life on earth: water, light, and, above all, agriculture. Locusts eat up all edible plant life, but also frogs, flies, wild animals, hail, and fire — all of these destroy the ecological conditions of life, and, in particular, human life.

But even this is not sufficient to distinguish plagues from other catastrophic events. What does, however, is the prominent role played by living creatures in the destruction of life, as epitomized by the locusts, frogs, flies, wild animals, lice, and gnats (fleas, we recall, played a major role in the transmission of the plague).

In short, what distinguishes the plague from other "natural" catastrophes is the degree to which it is the result of "life against life," or more concretely, of the living, of living beings, destroying life in general and human life in particular. This was true of the bubonic and pneumonic plagues, spread by living bacilli, and it is true today of Covid-19, if, as already suggested, we are willing to call into question the traditional determination of life as self-sustaining and extend it to the mode of reproduction of viruses, who require "hosts" in order to reproduce themselves.

For what is called "life" is, now as then, closely associated with the notion of self-reproduction; the question raised by viruses is whether such reproduction is entirely a function of a "self" — of an identifiable, individuated being — or whether it requires "preexisting conditions" that are not part of its makeup in order to survive.

In the Biblical account, the question is responded to in the most ambiguous, equivocal manner thinkable. Life on earth is understood to be the product and property of a Supreme Being who is as eternal as he is universal, while at the same time being entirely singular and self-identical: "I am who I am," he tells Moses, when asked for his name (sometimes translated as "I am who I will be," thus englobing time and the future within his singular self-identity) (Exod. 3:14). If man is described as created in the image of his creator, then initially, as we have seen, human life could be expected to consist in procreating and multiplying, free of the restriction of mortality. The latter only enters the Garden of Eden with the serpent, who appeals to the desire of Eve and Adam to be like their Creator (which in a certain sense they already are — or should be!). It is thus in trying to be what they already are and what therefore has no object — the knowledge not just of good but of evil — that evil comes into the world in the form of the expulsion from Eden and the introduction of mortality as a limiting condition of life.

The plagues visited upon the pharaoh and his people thus demonstrate the power of the Creator of Life to deprive the living of the conditions necessary for their life, which includes their procreation (hence the significance of killing the firstborn). Life is circulation, but when the rivers turn to blood, the ambiguity of that circulation is revealed: blood must be invisible to function as the support of life; when it becomes visible, as a river, it is already out of control, beyond its localization in singular living bodies, and thus a condition not of survival but of demise. But it is the demise of singular living beings as they are dissolved into a circulation that is greater than themselves, and thus that signals their destruction. Rivers of blood consist of blood shed, even if the violence that destroys individual bodies and sheds their blood is not visible.

It is significant that in describing how Covid-19 is spread, one also speaks of "shedding" the virus as a description of spreading it. The circulation of things and humans that is an essential part of life thus becomes a mechanism of spreading not life but death. Again, it is useful to recall that what is at stake in this demonstration of divine power is the decision of the pharaoh to release the people of Israel from their confinement in Egypt. If he does not let them go, the life of his people and his nation will be released from enabling limits and thus destroyed. The Biblical plagues, then, demonstrate not just the power of the divine Creator of all life, but even more the power of the living to destroy the living.

This notion of "the living destroying the living" requires further elucidation. If the plague combines both an external and an internal process in its operation, it resembles in this the life processes themselves. These are both internal and external, involving an interaction with the environment no less than a relatively self-contained procedure. The circulation of blood is a good example of this: it is, as the word itself suggests, circular, coursing through the body in a relatively fixed and finite trajectory. But it is also influenced by external forces, as most recently demonstrated by the ability of the virus, SARS-CoV-2 to enter the capillary cells via the ACE-2 receptor proteins. But in a less medical context, blood serves the functioning of living beings as long as it is retained within this internal trajectory: when blood exceeds the internal trajectory, it becomes a sign of the vulnerability of these bodies. The rivers that are turned to blood in the first of the plagues that the Hebrew God visits upon Egypt thus share with the plague — which in a strict sense they are not — the tendency of the circulation of life processes to exceed the boundaries set by finite living beings insofar as they are bodily beings, which is to say, spatially localized and limited. The transformation of river water into blood does not simply abolish localization but relocalizes while depriving it of the secure confines of bodily circulation; in so doing blood becomes the medium of death rather than of life. Here is how this lethal relocalization is described:

> And the LORD spake unto Moses, Say unto Aaron, Take thy rod and stretch out thine hand upon the waters of Egypt, upon their streams, upon their rivers, and upon their ponds, and upon all their pools of water, that they may become blood; and that there may be blood throughout all the land of Egypt, both in vessels of wood and in vessels of stone.... And the Egyptians could not drink of the water of the river; and there was blood throughout all the land of Egypt (Exod. 7:19–25).

Note the detail of the way the waters of the rivers, ponds, and pools in being turned into blood are still kept in "vessels": "vessels of wood and in vessels of stone." The liquid is still contained, just as blood is contained in living bodies, except that the bodies are no longer living. They are of stone and wood, but they do not provide the Egyptians with the liquid that is necessary for their lifeblood, as it were, with drinkable water.

What is suggested here is what we will discover in the more detailed accounts of the plague: first, that it always is localized, and second, that its localization no longer serves to further life but to destroy it. It moves from place to place, as it will move from body to body. And this indicates why the plague has to remain localized: for the site of its destructive force is the singular living body, whether human, animal, or vegetable. But it disrupts the integrity of those bodies, a disruption that often enough will be manifest by the shedding of blood or by the explosion of pustules on surface of the body.[3]

The divine plagues visited upon the Egyptians, like the plagues of more earthly origin, require bodies in order to function. But their operation mimics the movement of the life processes they destroy, whether the life process of individual living beings or of collective entities such as societies. And this is no accident, since the earthly plagues involve living processes that are directed against the survival of living organisms.

The fact that plagues require bodies to function brings us to another aspect of their operation: they seize upon individual living beings but are not limited to them qua individuals. The plague profits from the fact that singular living beings require interaction with others — with other living beings as with their environment, living or not — in order to exist. As with the divine plagues visited upon Egypt, plagues tend to replace an environment that is more or less propitious to life with one that is hostile to it. This predisposes the plague to the kind of "militarization" or "weaponization" that characterizes its appearance in the Old Testament, where it appears almost always as a means by which God seeks to punish his adversaries, usually to defend his adherents. Thus, for example, in the first book of Samuel, God sends a plague to punish the Philistines for having appropriated the Ark of the Covenant after their victory over Israel. The victors are finally constrained by the advent of "emerods" or "tumors" to return the Ark with supplementary sacrifices (golden effigies of the "emerods" and of mice) (1 Sam. 5–6). But it is not always the adversaries of his people who are punished by the plague. There is one case at least where God decides to punish the people with whom he has made a covenant, and that instance is recounted in the Second Book of Samuel.

What is of particular interest in our context is the relation that emerges in this episode between the plague and enumeration, for it is a motif that will recur again and again in the accounts of the plague we shall be reading. The Biblical situation is the following: King David decides that a census should be taken of the people of Israel and Judah, "that I may know the number of the people" (2 Sam. 24:2). As the story makes clear, the reason for this is largely military. David is engaged in a series of conflicts and wishes to know the human reserve he can mobilize. As in the first and decisive transgression in Genesis, here, too, a desire to acquire knowledge is expressed. The knowledge of good and evil is not involved in this story, but rather the knowledge of the number of his subjects by the earthly sovereign. In short, a certain kind of self-knowledge: the king wishing to count his subjects. The aim is not unrelated to that of Adam and Eve: they wish to acquire something of the immortality of their Creator (even if they have it already). David wishes to secure the survival of his kingdom and his people. But he is warned by Joab, his chief commander, that this is not the way to do it, for it incurs the wrath of the Lord of Life himself. Since this episode is recounted in a later part of the Old Testament, Chronicles, and since the later version of Joab's warning to David is more easily intelligible than the one in Samuel, I will quote it here:

> The Lord make his people an hundred times so many more as they be: but, my lord the king, are they not all my lord's servants? Why then doth my lord require this thing? (1 Chron. 21:3)[4]

In short, the number of the people falls not ultimately in the realm of earthly power, since "how many soever they be," the Lord can add "an hundredfold," and "the eyes of my lord the King" — i.e., David — "may see it" but not control it through knowledge of its momentary state. This, however, is precisely what David wants, mainly for military purposes — and this in turn has been seen as an anticipation of what later, in the reign of Solomon, will become a "cult of numbering" as Herbert Marks, editor of a recent edition of the King James Bible, describes it.[5] In order to preserve its own power, if not to augment it, earthly sovereignty depends upon enumeration, which however tends to hypostatize the givenness of the present, of that fixed moment of time when the enumeration is enacted. It thereby tends to ignore the significance of temporal change.

Once again, then, as in the Book of Genesis, we have a usurpation of divine prerogatives by earthly beings, and once again, this takes place in the name of acquiring a certain form of knowledge. But now it is not that of good and evil (an evil that is nonexistent in the Garden of Eden), but a knowledge of number: the number of men that can be used for military purposes. King David, compelled by what I would call the logic of earthly sovereignty to alienate his Creator by maintaining his decision, persists in his plan to hold the census, which significantly lasts almost the same period as that of the gestation of a human life, namely, nine months, or to be exact, "nine months and twenty days." At the end of this period, Joab is able to inform the king that "there were in Israel eight hundred thousand valiant men that drew the sword, and the men of Judah were five hundred thousand men" (2 Sam. 24:9).

Having thus succumbed to the temptation of assuring his earthly power as king, David is overcome by guilt at having defied his Sovereign. Cognizant of his sin, David begs the Lord for forgiveness. Speaking through the prophet Gad, the Lord offers the king a choice between three punishments, once again expressed in numerical terms, but this time involving a different form of enumeration:

> Shall seven years of famine come unto thee in thy land? Or wilt thou flee three months before thine enemies, while they pursue thee? Or that there be three days of pestilence in thy land? (2 Sam. 24:13)

The choices are once again numerical, but now not on the measure of individual persons but on time: seven years of famine, three months of flight, or three days of pestilence. David opts for the latter, and his reasoning will again resonate through the centuries: "Let us fall now into the hand of the Lord, for his mercies are great, and let me not fall into the hand of man" (2 Sam. 24:14). The plague as divine punishment may well be the most devastating, but it is also the shortest in time, and it holds out the possibility of a mercy that cannot easily be expected from human adversaries. David's calculation proves to be not entirely false:

> So the Lord sent a pestilence upon Israel from the morning even to the time appointed, and there died of the people from Dan even to Beersheba seventy thousand men. And when the angel stretched out his hand upon Jerusalem to destroy it, the Lord repented him of the evil and said to the angel that destroyed the people, it is enough, stay now thine hand. (2 Sam. 24:15)

These episodes from the Old Testament introduce a relation that will resonate throughout the history of plagues and pandemics, up until today: the relation between illness and number. The plague is not just an individual illness, but a collective malady. It strikes individuals, and thus is susceptible to enumeration. But it strikes them as members of a large collective: a locality, a society, an ethnic, racial, or socioeconomic group. This makes the tendency to enumerate inevitable but also unreliable and problematic for there will persist a chasm that separates the death of singular living beings from its reduction to a number in a list. This chasm is precisely what will render the project of enumeration as reassuring as it is frightening. For if enumeration is intrinsically interminable, the lives of those it recounts are not. It is this discrepancy between the ability to count indefinitely, and the uncountable life and death of singular beings that will demand that the plague not merely be counted, but recounted.

CHAPTER THREE

Polytheistic Antecedents:

The Plague as Stasis

(Thucydides)

Already in the preceding discussion of the episodes from the Old Testament, it is clear that one of the major aspects of "the plague" involves its "weaponization" as a means of demonstrating power and intervening in conflicts. But as long as the wielder of this weapon is also the Creator of the Universe, the struggle cannot be among equals. There is no equilibrium to be achieved, no negotiations, only submission to a power beyond all measure. But it is nevertheless a power that works by using the processes through which life itself operates: circulation, exchange, communication. This is what distinguishes the plague from other cataclysmic catastrophes, which strike more or less from without (astral collisions), or which when emanating from within the earth, still do not directly utilize the processes by which living organisms live and reproduce. This also holds for the plague as divine retribution, punishment, or simply demonstration of power: its initial source may be the Creator of the Universe and of its life, but that source itself remains separate from the life it affects and sometimes destroys. The plague emanates from the source of all life, but in contrast to other catastrophes, it uses living beings and the conditions of life themselves to threaten other living beings, including (but not necessarily exclusively) human beings, both individually and collectively. This is what justifies the formula defining the plague as the lethal attack of the living against the living, of life against life.

But the relationship of the plague to life, as its source and as its target, is also what distinguishes the plague from ordinary forms of war — to which the plague throughout its history will repeatedly be compared, up until today.[1] What makes the comparison of plagues and pandemics with wars so attractive is, above all, the collective nature of the threat they both embody: they strike down not just individuals, but also groups, collectives. Any collective mobilization, therefore, has been marketed in recent decades as a "war": the Cold War, the War on Poverty (Lyndon Johnson), the war on drugs, and, of course, most recently, the war on terror. In all of these cases, however, the extended use of the term war has diverged from its classical form. Traditionally, wars involved more or less protracted conflicts between politically organized entities, classically involving "declarations" of war at the opening of hostilities and then concluding with some sort of mutual agreement: armistice, surrender, truce. The operation of the war was also, at certain times, organized by previously existing agreements, the so-called rules of war, relating to the treatment of prisoners, of civilians, forbidding the use of certain types of weapons, etc. That such agreements were often ignored during the conflicts themselves does not negate the obligations they imply, which can lead to partial if imperfect observation by warring parties.[2]

To be sure, the nature of armed conflict has changed greatly with social, political, and technological developments, starting in the nineteenth century and persisting until today. As Carl Schmitt has emphasized in his study of guerilla warfare, the "irregular" nature of popular, anti-colonial revolts made it ever more difficult to submit such conflicts to generally applicable rules, especially given the dissymmetry of the conflicting parties: on the one hand, a constituted national political entity, usually a nation-state, and on the other, far more informal popular groupings of guerillas (from the Spanish *guerrilla*: "little war").[3] The equivalent word in other Romance languages and in German, however, reflects a more specific type of "warrior" — *partisan, partigiano, Partisanen* — since the words derive from the word for "party," which is both part of a whole (unlike the state, which claims at least to represent the whole), and also suggests adherence to an ideology, a set of ideals, rather than an established organization.

Despite this historical shift in the concept of "war," from regulated conflict between nation-states to "asymmetrical" conflicts between state institutions (army, police, militias) and "irregular" armed groups, the very notion of war, like the concept of law, to which it is traditionally related, both presuppose something that is strangely absent from the operation of plagues and pestilences: self-conscious, deliberate planning at the origin of action. Such planning, in turn, links goal-directed activity to conscious intentionality. This link, however, is precisely what pandemics call into question. Bacteria, and even more perhaps viruses, operate in a highly complex goal-directed manner, seeking to reproduce themselves by taking over the host's reproductive mechanisms. Conspiratorial theories in general, and in the case of Covid-19 in particular, seek to compensate for this uncanny divergence between goal-directed activity and self-conscious planning by searching for an original "planner," for instance, the Wuhan Institute for Virology, and in particular its P4 laboratory.[4] The desire to find a "human" intentional and deliberate cause of a pandemic does not tell us anything about the likelihood of such a process taking place. It only demonstrates that the effort to find such an origin could serve to reduce the anxiety triggered by the possibility that such destructiveness could be the result of pure chance, or of mechanisms that as such would be entirely beyond human control.[5] An alternative explanation could recognize human activity to be the source of the pandemic, for instance, by altering the biosphere, but it would be an activity with only a short-term vision of the consequences of such alterations.

The inability to identify a clearly defined self-consciousness governing the progress of a pandemic is thus one of the defining characteristics of the experience of plagues in the modern period, at least; this contrasts with the conception of plagues as a means by which God punishes iniquitous humanity. This attitude presupposes a belief in a divinity governing earthly events and distributing justifiable retribution—a belief that has, in many areas, greatly diminished, although it has by no means disappeared.

This inability to discern a first cause or a final purpose of plagues, combined with their collective character invites comparison with "war." This comparison is tempting but also generally short-lived, as it becomes clear that the ravages of the pandemic do not follow a master plan, or at least not one that reflects a governing self-consciousness.

And yet, as we shall discover shortly, the account of the plague given by Thucydides in his *History of the Peloponesian Wars,* both confirms the difference between it and the war being fought between Athens and Sparta, while at the same time suggesting a different comparison: not with interstate war, but with civil war, a war that is both internal and external at the same time.[6] The violence of such a conflict knows no limits (including that separating internal from external).

To get a sense of how decisive the question of self-consciousness, on a collective scale, is in the relation of the war to the plague, we need only reread that portion of Book 2 in which the account of the plague ravaging Athens is sandwiched between the two major discourses of Pericles: first, the so-called funeral oration, and second, the discourse encouraging the Athenians to continue the conflict with Sparta despite the ravages of the plague.

Pericles spends very little time speaking about those who have fallen in the war. He is fulfilling an Athenian custom in commemorating them, Thucydides writes, but his account makes clear that this is not really his main concern. "What I want to do is, in the first place, to discuss the spirit in which we faced our trials ... and the way of life that has made us great" (2:36). He begins by praising the traditions handed down by the ancestors of the Athenians:

> In this land of ours there have always been the same people living from generation to generation up till now and they, by their courage and virtue, have handed it on to us, a free country (2:36).

In sum, individual Athenians will come and go. Singular living beings are mortal, whether they die in war, or of illness, or of old age. But what does not change is the collective culture to which they all belong. In other words, the generational change is acknowledged, but generational differences do not constitute a "break" or discontinuity; above and beyond the coming and going of singular, mortal Athenians, a social continuum is appealed to that would outlive individual mortality: Athenians as a group remain the same, despite generational change. This sameness is defined and conveyed through the relatively durable traditions, customs, and institutions of Athens. Athenian democracy is described as "free and open.... free and tolerant in our private lives, but in public affairs we keep to the law" (2:37). However, it is only in the Crawley translation that English readers discover just how and why the Athenians "keep to the law," as Warner puts it, despite the relative openness of their private lives:

> But all this ease in our private relations does not make us lawless as citizens. Against this, awe [deos] is our chief safeguard, teaching us to obey the magistrates and the laws (2:37).[7]

Thucydides acknowledges *deos* — "awe," "respect," but in the sense of the German *Ehrfurcht*, fear of what deserves honor — as the decisive factor in bridging the gap between a more or less permissive private life and a more or less rigorous, law-abiding public one. As its etymology suggests, it results from a split, a "duo,"[8] as with the German word *Zweifel* (from *zwei*). Although Pericles does not really explain the source or object of this "awe," he does give an example that is telling:

> Against this, fear (awe) is our chief safeguard, teaching us to obey the magistrates and the laws, particularly such as regard the protection of the wronged [*ton adikoumenon*, "those denied justice"] (2:37).

A certain "fear" or "respect" — *déos* — serves as a "safeguard" by teaching the Athenians to respect laws insofar as they protect citizens from injustice. As we shall see, when the plague ravages the city, it destroys the "safeguard" and with it, obedience to the law. But here Pericles is not thinking of the plague, which will take him and the Athenians fully by surprise. Instead, he is laying the groundwork to explain the superiority of Athenian culture over that of Sparta, which he seeks also to demonstrate in respect to the organization of "military security." Here again, Athens is described as "open to the world," without having to resort to "periodical deportations" or "secret weapons... because we rely on our own real courage and loyalty" (2:39). In comparing the Athenian educational system to that of the Spartans, Pericles emphasizes that the Athenians do not need to submit themselves to the same "laborious training" or "restrictions," since even without them, "we are just as ready to face the same dangers as they are" (2:39). And he continues,

> There are certain advantages... in our way of meeting danger voluntarily.... We do not have to spend our time practicing to meet sufferings which are still in the future; and when they are actually upon us we show ourselves just as brave as these others who are always in strict training.... We are capable at the same time of taking risks and of estimating them beforehand. Others are brave out of ignorance; and, when they stop to think, they begin to fear. But the man who most truly can be accounted brave is he who best knows the meaning of what is sweet in life and of what is terrible, and then goes out undeterred to meet what is to come. (2:39–40)

To resume, Pericles praises the Athenians for not needing the training, discipline, and restraint that the Spartans practice. It is enough to "know the meaning of what is sweet in life and what is terrible" to be able to confront "what is to come." In particular, he is contemptuous of the way "fear" intervenes in their behavior. For the Athenians, fear provokes thought and reflection; for the Spartans, he asserts, it is the other way around: "When they stop to think, they begin to fear." The result is that the Athenians need not fear the future as must the Spartans, because they can counter it with a general knowledge, of the sweet and the terrible in life, a knowledge that is sufficient to allow them to "meet what is to come."

Contrast this evaluation with the way Thucydides describes the actions of the Spartans at the outbreak of the plague:

> At the beginning of the summer following [the funeral oration], the Pelopon-
> nesians and their allies . . . invaded Attica. . . . Taking up their positions, they
> set about devastating the country.
>
> They had not been many days in Attica before the plague first broke out
> among the Athenians. . . . The plague broke out directly after the Pelopon-
> nesian invasion, and never affected the Peloponnese at all, or not seriously; its
> full force was felt at Athens, and after Athens, in the most densely populated
> of the other towns. (2:54)

The plague notwithstanding, Pericles organizes an attack against the Peloponnesians, while the invaders were still in Attica, devastating areas under Athenian control. The Athenians do the same, before returning home, to find

> that the Peloponnesians had also retired and were no longer in Attica. . . .
> Indeed it was said that the Peloponnesians left Attica earlier than they had
> intended because they were afraid of the infection. (2:57)

In short, the Peloponnesians did not hesitate to change their plans and withdraw earlier than foreseen because of the significance they attached to their "fear" of the plague, precisely what Pericles had derided in his characterization of their "bravery." Thus, they are able to maintain the health of their armies in contrast to the Athenians, who do not hesitate to launch military operations while the plague is at its height, thus increasingly debilitating their military as well as their civilians.

Fear is a way of acknowledging both the unpredictability of the future and one's potential vulnerabilities. Spartan discipline and training, scorned by Pericles, enable them to acknowledge their fear and to act effectively upon it, by withdrawing to a less-threatened place. By contrast, the Athenians faith in the power of their intelligence and confidence in their ability to meet every danger spontaneously, "naturally" as it were, exposes themselves all the more to the ravages of the plague and impedes their ability to wage war successfully. Thucydides demonstrates the inappropriateness of the Athenian attitude by emphasizing how the virulence of the plague appeared to be entirely unprecedented (reminiscent of the initial reaction to the "novel coronavirus," Covid-19):

> There was no record of the disease being so virulent anywhere else or causing so many deaths as it did in Athens. At the beginning the doctors were quite incapable of treating the disease because of their ignorance of the right methods. . . . Nor was any other human art or science of any help at all. Equally useless were prayers made in the temples, consultation of oracles and so forth. In the end people were so overcome by their suffering that they paid no further attention to such things. (2:47)[9]

Whereas the speech of Pericles stressed the capacity of the Athenians to confront any danger whatsoever, Thucydides' description of the intensity and novelty of the plague provides a cruel response to Pericles:

> Words indeed fail one when one tries to give a general picture of this disease; and as for the sufferings of individuals, they seemed almost beyond the capacity of human nature to endure. Here in particular is a point where this plague showed itself to be something quite different from ordinary diseases. . . . As for a recognized method of treatment, it would be true to say that no such thing existed: what did good in some cases did harm in others. (2:50)

Contrast Thucydides' emphasis on the inability of language to express the horrors of the plague with Pericles's confident assertion that "We Athenians . . . do not think that there is an incompatibility between words and deeds" (2:40). Words are the indispensable medium for the formulation of general concepts, and hence a decisive element of that "natural" anticipation of danger that Pericles ascribes to the Athenian genius. But precisely such words "fail . . . to give a general picture of this disease," since its unprecedented ferocity defies all attempts at subsuming it under previously familiar generalizations. This is also why, according to Thucydides, "a recognized treatment" could not be found, since "what did good in some cases did harm in others." In other words, the plague demonstrates an irreducibly *singular* characteristic: different persons respond differently to the same treatment.

In short, the plague makes a mockery of Pericles's evaluation of the Athenian ability to face up to dangers without submitting to the discipline, training, and above all, prudence of Spartan culture. Whereas the Spartans acknowledge fear as that which resists generalization, the Athenians are left defenseless when confronted with its unprecedented force:

> The most terrible thing of all was the despair into which people fell when they realized that they had caught the plague; for they would immediately adopt an attitude of utter hopelessness, and, by giving in in this way, would lose their power of resistance. (2:51)

It is worth noting that in the several pages that Thucydides devotes to describing the ravages of the plague, he says nothing about the presence of any sort of organization or government. It is as if the total inability of the Athenians to anticipate an unprecedented future left them no alternative other than trying to respond to the plague entirely as individuals. But here, too, the plague seems to have the last word. For where people try to help each other as individuals, they often fall victim to the plague themselves. There is no mention in Thucydides of any organized resistance or countermeasures to the plague, only disorganization. Funeral ceremonies "were now disorganized," and people "buried the dead as best they could" (2:52). Given this absence of public organization, it is hardly surprising that there develops "the beginnings of a state of unprecedented lawlessness.... No fear of god or law of man had a restraining influence," since no one expected to live long enough to suffer punishment for violating the laws. As for religion, "it seemed to be the same . . . whether one worshipped . . . or not, when one saw the good and the bad dying indiscriminately" (2:53). The only mention of governmental activity noted by Thucydides are two ill-fated military expeditions organized by Pericles against the Peloponnesians, during which "the plague broke out" among the Athenian troops, "with the most disastrous effects on the army" (2:58).

As a result of these disasters, Thucydides describes how public opinion begins to turn against Pericles, who is held responsible for the catastrophic ineffectiveness of the state, and peace feelers are sent out to the Spartans by his aristocratic critics. This results then in the second great speech of Pericles, in which he defends his policies and tries to remobilize the Athenians for the war. His discourse involves, above all, convincing them that their personal safety, greatly threatened by the plague and the military defeats, is impossible to separate from the security of the *polis*. And in the particular case of Athens, the security of the city-state, as Pericles asserts, is inseparable from the defense of the empire it has built through its maritime forces. Pericles alternates his appeal to the Athenians between the carrot and the stick. The carrot consists in reminding them of their great imperial accomplishments and traditions, of their cultural and mental superiority to their enemies, of their "intelligence" that enables them not only "to look down on [their] opponents [with contempt]" (*kataphronêmati*) but "by estimating what the facts are" to "obtain a clearer vision of what to expect" (2:62).

To be sure, Pericles has already acknowledged that "a great and sudden disaster has fallen upon you" and as a result "you have weakened in carrying out to the end the resolves which you made. When things happen suddenly, unexpectedly, and against all calculation, it subjugates the spirit [*douloi gar phronêma*]" (2:61). But Pericles presents this situation primarily as a private disaster on the part of individuals rather than as the result of a flawed political policy and culture. He does not offer any explanation of how the previously praised Athenian "intelligence" could have been responsible for the inability to organize a collective and effective response to "the unexpected event" of the plague. If the plague is one of those events that occurs "against all calculation," then this could suggest that something more and other than mere calculation is required if its destructive effects are to be countered. This, for instance, will be one of the considerations informing Defoe's *Journal of the Plague Year*. But it is not the main concern of Pericles. On the contrary, he concludes his oration — at least in the version communicated by Thucydides — with an appeal to the greatness of Athens that at the same time acknowledges that it is not just living individuals who are mortal, but also the collectives to which they belong:

> Remember, too, that the reason why Athens has the greatest name in all the
> world is because she has never given in to adversity, but has spent more life and
> labor in warfare than any other state, thus winning the greatest power that
> has ever existed in history, such a power that will be remembered for ever by
> posterity, even if now (since all things are born to decay) there should come a
> time when we were forced to yield. (2:64)

Pericles thus acknowledges that even the greatest power in the world, which he attributes to Athens, cannot overcome mortality, "since all things are born to decay" and especially all living things. He therefore appeals to memory as a consolation. And we must "remember" that the text we are reading has done much to preserve the memory of Athens and its self-inflicted downfall, at least in relation to its conflict with Sparta.

But it is not simply the memory of "the greatest power that has ever existed in history" that is memorialized in Thucydides's *History*. Rather, it is also the fact that even the greatest of powers is vulnerable to the extent that it does not acknowledge its limitations and tries to compensate for them other than by imperial expansion. For power, far from eliminating constraints, creates new ones — and with them, new vulnerabilities. Pericles is well aware of this, and this is "the stick" that accompanies the "carrot" he extends to the Athenians. If they constitute the greatest power in the world at the time, this is due to an empire that also imposes both obligations and constraints:

> It is right and proper for you to support the imperial dignity of Athens. . . . You
> cannot continue to enjoy the privileges unless you also shoulder the burdens

of empire. Do not imagine that what we are fighting for is simply ... freedom or slavery: there is also involved the loss of our empire and the dangers arising from the hatred that we have incurred in administering it. It is no longer possible for you to give up this empire. ... Your empire is now like a tyranny: it may have been wrong to take it; it is certainly dangerous to let it go. And the kind of people who talk of doing so ... would very soon bring a state to ruin. (2:63)

The Athenians are thus prisoners of the very power and privilege of Empire that they have established through conquest and commerce. Empire means both rule and subjugation, and the latter, when practiced entirely in the interests of the imperial power, produces "hatred" that can ultimately endanger its survival. In short, from the imperialist perspective, which is that of Athens, the preservation of freedom or autonomy — *eleutheria* — depends both on maintaining and expanding its domination in order to better defend itself. But because "all things are born to decay," such expansion involves a never-ending and ultimately fruitless struggle. And this holds for Empires as well as for individuals.[10]

In other words, at the heart of Pericles' exhortation is the attempt to give earthly, temporal, mortal existence a meaning that transcends its intrinsic limitations. Power is at the heart of his argument, although not just military and naval power is intended, but an intellectual, cultural, and political power. This power consists in the capacity to control and channel the passage of time in which "all things are born to decay." But it is precisely the plague that decisively upsets this project because it is totally incalculable, as incalculable as mortality itself.[11] This is its essential difference from war. In war, the aim is to control mortality by inflicting death upon the enemy and thereby subjugating it. War is planned violence, although from the very beginning of Thucydides's *History*, the limits of such calculability are constantly being stressed, as when the Athenian emissaries to Sparta warn the Spartans not to rush into conflict with them:

Take time, then, over your decision, which is an important one. ... Think ... of the great part that is played by the unpredictable in war: think of it now, before you are actually committed to war. The longer a war lasts, the more things tend to depend on accidents. Neither you nor we can see into them: we have to abide their outcome in the dark. (1:78)

These words of caution are almost immediately relayed by the Spartan king, Archidamus, "a man who had a reputation for both intelligence and moderation":

> Spartans, in the course of my life I have taken part in many wars, and I see among you people of the same age as I. They and I have had experience, and so are not likely to share in what may be a general enthusiasm for war. . . . (1:80)
>
> . . . We are taught that there is not a great deal of difference between the way we think and the way others think, and that it is impossible to calculate accurately events that are determined by chance. The practical measures that we take are always based on the assumption that our enemies are not unintelligent. And it is right and proper for us to put our hopes in the reliability of our own precautions rather than in the possibility of our opponent making mistakes. . . . (1:84)
>
> Let us never give up this discipline which our fathers have handed down to us and which we still preserve. . . . Let us not be hurried *kath'esuchian* [Crawley: let us deliberate at our leisure] . . . . We ought to take time over such a decision. (1:85)

"Let us take time over such a decision," is the advice of the older, experienced warrior and king, Archidamus. Later, in Book 6, the "young men" of Athens will be "roused" by the young and energetic Alcibiades to send a navy to Sicily. Here, however, the king is promptly overruled by the simpler call to action of the ephor (or "overseer," member of the ruling executive of Sparta), Sthenelaidas. Nevertheless, Archidamus's words demonstrate from a very different angle what Pericles derides as the "discipline" of the Spartans. Discipline, involving restraint but also reflection, is precisely a means of dealing with the incalculable based on respect both for the adversary and on recognition of the limitations of human intelligence to anticipate the future. Discipline here does not, however, mean the blind obedience to rules,[12] but rather restraint of tendencies to overvalue one's intelligence and power and to undervalue the need to reflect and deliberate before taking action. This need implics the willingness not to rush headlong into momentous decisions, but rather "to take time," to allow oneself time to consider, rather than out of unacknowledged anxiety to try to neutralize time, as the medium of the incalculable, through speed in attempting to attain one's goal. To "take time" here means to allow time to intervene between intention and action, desire and accomplishment, as the Corinthian case against the Athenians, outlined below, confirms. In recounting the warning of Archidamus, Thucydides acknowledges the enabling limits of all calculability and anticipation.

This is why it is not fortuitous that Archidamus begins by calling attention to his age, to the ages of many in the audience, and to the "experience" that this age can bring. Age *can* bring experience by acknowledging precisely the unpredictability of temporal change and the potentially destructive consequences of overcompensating for that unpredictability by rushing into decisions in order to avoid the anxieties provoked by an uncertain future and by the never fully calculable certitude of mortality.

If war, then, appears as a way of reducing that uncertainty, at least temporarily, this is precisely not the case with the plague, which, as we have seen, dissolves all certainties and hope for controlling the future. This is what separates war in its traditional form from the plague. But there is a form of war that closely resembles the plague and reminds us about some of its essential characteristics: not the war between states and empires, but civil war, the war that shatters the unity of the state or the *polis*. This can be seen in Thucydides's account of the civil war that ravages Corcyra (3:69–85).

Corcyra, a city on the island of Corfu, was an ally of Athens. During the war, a revolution broke out in a part of the city that, hoping to ally with Sparta, rose up against the pro-Athenian government, which was accused of being too subservient to Athens. Returning prisoners of the Spartan ally, Corinth, sought to detach Corcyra from Athens, and thereby ignited a struggle that quickly became violent, assassinating the ruling council of some sixty persons and calling on the people of the city to revolt in order "to prevent the island being enslaved by Athens" (3:71). Soon the Corinthian allies of Sparta arrived in a warship and helped the revolt to take control of the city. Thucydides describes in great detail the increasing violence and brutality that soon engulfed the city, with alternating intervention of Athenian and Spartan warships. He relates efforts both to control the situation and to maneuver, but all of this merely contributes to a state of growing confusion and brutal conflict. Here an example:

> The Corcyraeans were now in a state of the utmost confusion, alarmed both at what was happening inside their city and at the approach of the enemy fleet. They immediately got ready sixty ships and sent them straight out against the enemy.... As the Corcyraean ships approached the enemy in this disorganized way, two of them immediately deserted, in other ships the crews were fighting among themselves, and no sort of order was kept in anything (3:77).

The rise of such disorder, with the alternate coming and going of Peloponnesian and Athenian fleets and interventions, finally results in an explosion of killing that no longer observes any limits:

> When the Corcyraeans realized that the Athenian fleet was approaching and that their enemies had gone ... they seized upon all the enemies they could find and put them to death. They then dealt with those whom they had persuaded to go on board the ships, killing them as they landed. Next they went to the temple of Hera and persuaded about fifty of the suppliants there to submit to a trial. They then condemned every one of them to death. Seeing what was happening, most of the other suppliants, who had refused to be tried, killed each other there in the temple.... During seven days ... the Corcyraeans continued to massacre those of their own citizens whom they considered to be their enemies.... There was death in every shape and form. And, as usually happens in such situations, people went to every extreme and beyond it. There were fathers who killed their sons; men were dragged from the temples or butchered on the very altars; some were actually walled up in the temple of Dionysus and died there (3:81).

As usual in such situations, "people went to every extreme and beyond it." The situation in many ways resembles that brought about by the plague: the breakdown of all order under the pressure of increasing violence and death. And like the plague, the civil war operates simultaneously from without — the Athenian and Peloponnesian interventions — and from within, the struggle between the so-called democratic (pro-Athenian) faction rowers and the revolting oligarchical (pro-Spartan) landowners.

But there is still at least one significant difference: the plague kills and maims without direct intention; it merely exploits the mortal vulnerability of all living things, especially in their irreducible singularity. The civil war, by contrast, is still conducted in the name of general political goals and programs, although Thucydides is skeptical as to their effective force:

> Love of victory [philonikein], operating through greed [pleonexia] and through love of glory [philotimia], was the cause of all these evils. To this must be added the violent fanaticism which came into play once the struggle had broken out. Leaders of parties in the cities had programs that appeared admirable — on the one side political equality for the masses, on the other the safe and sound government of the aristocracy — but in professing to serve the public interest they were seeking to win the prizes [athla] for themselves (3:82; translation modified).

"Love of victory" and "love of glory" suggest that underneath the "admirable" public pronouncements, what was at work was the attempt to increase the power and wealth of private individuals. However, is this "love of glory" strictly personal, or is it the effort to compensate for the anxieties that are inseparable from the mortal existence of singular living beings? In which case, the effects of the plague in contributing to the destruction and defeat of Athens would be at least parallel to the debilitating effects of civil strife:

> Thus every form of iniquity took root in the Hellenic countries by reason of the troubles. The ancient simplicity into which honor so largely entered was laughed down and disappeared; and society became divided into camps in

which no man trusted his fellow. As for ending this state of affairs, no guarantee could be given that would be trusted, no oath sworn that people would fear to break.... As a rule those who were least remarkable for intelligence showed the greatest powers of survival. Such people recognized their own deficiencies... fearing that they might lose a debate... they boldly launched straight into action, while their opponents, overconfident in the belief that they would see what was happening in advance... were the more easily destroyed because they were off their guard (3:83–84).

Just as the situation of polarized conflict allowed for "no guarantee" that this "state of affairs" could be ended, the plague, too, offers no guarantee that the devastation it produces can be brought to a clear-cut end — and that it might not return in an even more devastating form.

One of the results is to favor a survival of "the fittest," whereby being "fit" converges with being able to fuse power with action. But it is an action that tends to confirm the destructive and lethal effects of power, rather than attenuating them.

An alternative possibility can perhaps be glimpsed some 1,700 years later, when a similar plague ravages a city not so far removed from Athens, but produces a very different response.

CHAPTER FOUR

Storytelling as Friction

(Boccaccio, *The Decameron*)

Written in the middle of the fourteenth century (1349–1353) Boccaccio's *Decameron* is situated historically on the cusp of a European society transitioning from a fundamentally religious view of the world to a more secular, earthly experience. Already the title chosen by Boccaccio, *Decameron*, echoes an earlier work by the Christian theologian Saint Ambrose, entitled *Hexaemeron*. But the echo, as scholars have noted, is highly ironic.[1] St. Ambrose's work is an elaboration on the creation of the world as recounted in the first book of Genesis, which was accomplished in six days, the seventh being reserved for rest. In contrast, Boccaccio's *Decameron* also recounts a kind of creation of a world, but it is a world of storytelling, and so the creation is really a re-creation, in the many senses of that word. Nothing "real" is created, since with one important exception, all the characters are fictional. (I will come back to the exception in a moment.) But not only are the characters fictional: to a large extent, the stories they tell are adapted from already existing stories (here, too, we will discuss one important exception later on). So the *Decameron* does not recount the creation of *the world* — the one and only world by a one and only creator — but rather of *a* world that is not really a world but an escape from the world. Boccaccio, as he himself will insist at the end of the *Decameron*, is not God, but only an author — and as we shall see, not even an author, but a writer, a kind of scribe, reinscribing previous stories and thereby placing them in a new and different context.

Boccaccio cannot create the world, for it already exists, and as previously mentioned, it is caught up in a process of rapid and fundamental change. But this change brings with it terrible suffering. Although an economic recovery commenced at the beginning of the fourteenth century, it was accompanied by widespread famine (1313–1315); then in 1347, one of the most devastating plagues reached Europe, arriving first in Genoa and one year later reaching the city of Florence. This plague would ravage the city for three years, during which time it would take the lives of about half of its population, if not more (the statistics are all estimates). At the same time that it began to spread all over Europe, it also raged in North Africa and the Middle East and so became a true pandemic. Today, it is considered one, if not the, most fatal of pandemics, claiming the lives of anywhere between seventy to two hundred million people worldwide.

This, then, was the world that provides the setting for Boccaccio's *Decameron*. If the Bible insists that the world created by God was "good, very good," the same could hardly be said for the world of the fourteenth century. For religious believers, whether Christian or Muslim, the plague was sent by God either to punish or to test his creatures. But for those for whom a transcendent God was becoming less important than life on earth, this was not much of a consolation.

Boccaccio not only wrote in this world; he explicitly inscribed it in his *Decameron*. The question I will be addressing in this chapter is simply: Why? Why did he choose to use plague-struck Florence as the point of departure for the one hundred stories that compose the *Decameron* — told over a period of ten days, hence the title. Boccaccio himself will, of course, address this question and try to justify his choice, but his explanation is not entirely convincing, and it requires readers to think further for themselves. This is what I will try to do in the following pages.

The text begins with a short preface and then a longer introduction by the author. The preface emphasizes the importance of

compassion in the life of the author, who confesses that he only survived because of the help given him by his friends. He acknowledges
that he was passionately in love and that he was only saved from the
self-destructive effects of his uncontrolled passions by the intervention of friends. This made him realize the importance of compassion, feeling for others, and his decision to write the *Decameron* is an
attempt to repay his debt and encourage compassion among his readers. In particular, he addresses himself to women, whom he asserts
are marginalized from active life by a male-dominated society and
are forced to stay at home. Through the reading of the stories he will
recount, he hopes that the ladies will have not only pleasure "but useful advice as well" (5).

But in the longer introduction that follows this short preface,
where the author declares his intention to please and to counsel,
a problem arises. That problem is the plague that is devastating
Florence at the very time that Boccaccio is writing the *Decameron*,
namely, 1348 to 1351. Rather than ignoring this fact, Boccaccio insists
on it, and therefore, he has to explain why he is presenting the stories
against the dark background of the plague:

> Most gracious ladies, whenever I contemplate how compassionate you all are
> by nature, I recognize that, in your judgment, the present work will seem
> both somber and painful, for its opening contains the sad record of the recent,
> deadly plague (5).

Although this "sad record" has provoked "horror and pity in all who
actually saw it," Boccaccio insists that it is absolutely indispensable
that readers keep this in memory if they are to appreciate the true
significance of the stories he is about to tell:

> Without recalling these events, I could not explain the origins of the things
> you will read about later on. I have been forced by necessity to write it all
> down (5).

What Boccaccio is referring to here is the situation that will frame
his one hundred stories, namely, the meeting of the seven women

and three men in the Church of Santa Maria Novella — a church that exists today in Florence. Scholars speculate this site was chosen by Boccaccio as the meeting place perhaps because of its name, "Novella," since what is going to emerge from the meeting of the seven women and three men is precisely the telling of stories, *novelle*, over ten days.[2] So fiction and reality are closely allied from the very beginning to the end of the *Decameron*: in a perfectly fictional manner, the women and men, all of whom have fictitious names, meet in a recognizably real church and decide to flee Florence for the countryside where they will recreate a community as a temporary alternative to the one that is in the process of being destroyed by the plague. Over ten days, these ten persons will live together, with their servants to be sure, thus continuing the social hierarchy of the city they leave behind them, but also establishing rules of conduct that they, by and large, adhere to while they tell each other stories during the time they spend together.

But although Boccaccio insists that it is necessary for him to show how these stories emerge from the plague-ridden city, he never really explains why this is necessary or even how it could be so. The stories themselves make no direct reference to the plague, but deal with all aspects of human and social relations. The question then is why should the plague need to frame these stories and what does it signify for them? As frame, the plague sets the scene for the storytelling that will occupy the *Decameron*; it poses the question of the relation between storytelling, between narration, and the terrible events narrated at its outset, which also constitute a kind of story, although not one that can simply be qualified as "fictional." Since the notion of "fiction" as generally used seems to presuppose that it can be opposed to "reality" in a mutually exclusive opposition, I want to suggest that the two interpenetrate one another in the *Decameron*: the stories take place in recognizably "real" places, even if they do not simply reproduce real events. And real events cast a long shadow over all the stories, as we shall see. Therefore, instead of seeing the frame as a "real" reference enclosing non-real, "fictional" stories, I want to suggest that the relation between the plague and the storytelling is not one of reality to fiction, but one that encompasses both. For storytelling has its own reality, and even if it is not the same as the reality it represents, it is also not unrelated to it, nor to its frame. Rather, the relationship between frame and story — whether of the plague itself or of the myriad events in the stories that follow — can therefore be better qualified as "frictional."[3] One thing "rubs up" against the next, and in the process, both are transformed. This is the general pattern of what I am calling "friction." I will try to explain its implications as we proceed. Historically, I will add that the transitional world in which and of which Boccaccio writes "rubs up" against the previous religious attitude emphasizing transcendence and brings it down to earth. This process is the condition for the kind of "friction" I will be interpreting.

Why should it have been necessary, as Boccaccio puts it at the outset, for the reader to follow a path that starts with the plague in order to lead beyond it, where "there lies a most beautiful and delightful plain" (5)? Boccaccio justifies this first claim with a Biblical allusion: "Just as happiness at its limit turns into sadness, so misery is ended by the joy that follows it" (5). Scholars have indicated that this is an allusion to the Old Testament, namely, to a verse from Proverbs 14:13 (5). But Boccaccio's relation to tradition — whether to the Bible, as here, or to Dante, as throughout — is precisely what I am calling "frictional." He rubs up against it, which is to say, he interacts with and depends on certain "transcendent" notions, while not being able to offer a religiously transcendent justification of them. This forces him to modify his religious sources to conform with a more problematic earthly situation. Here, he modifies the Biblical verse, which, in the King James Version of the Bible, reads: "Even in laughter the heart is sorrowful, and the end of that mirth is heaviness." And if we read the verse that precedes this one in Proverbs, we find that it emphasizes the somber outcome: "There is a way which seemeth right unto a man but the end thereof are the ways of death" (Prov. 14:12). The situation that Boccaccio invokes to situate his stories would seem to be closer to Proverbs than his own reformulation would suggest. Except that even in his reformulation, the "joy" that ends "misery" still remains subject to the limit of a happiness that ultimately turns into "sadness." Despite Boccaccio's attempts to justify beginning the *Decameron* with the plague—and despite his argument that, although happiness may turn into sadness, misery will end in joy—nothing he writes really contradicts the Proverbs' gloomy insistence that "the end of mirth is heaviness" and that the end of human ways is death. In short, by adapting this verse from the Old Testament, Boccaccio questions the promise announced by the New Testament. Beyond "the mountain" (of the plague), lies not eternal life but death.

This very somber reinterpretation of the Christian promise of redemption is reinforced when we see how Boccaccio begins his account of the plague:

> One thousand, three hundred and forty-eight years had passed since the fruitful Incarnation of the Son of God when the deadly plague arrived in the noble city of Florence. . . . Whether it descended on us mortals through the influence of the heavenly bodies or was sent down by God in His righteous anger to chastise us because of our wickedness . . . it moved relentlessly from place to place. Against it all human wisdom and foresight were useless. . . . Nor were the humble supplications made to God by the pious . . . any more effective (5–6).

The dating of the plague with reference to "the fruitful Incarnation of the Son of God" some 1,400 years before takes on a particularly sinister significance in view of the distinctive way the plague "incarnates" itself; it can be read as a lethal parody of Christian resurrection:

> The plague began producing its sad effects in a terrifying and extraordinary manner: It did not operate as it had done in the East, where if anyone bled through the nose it was a clear sign of inevitable death. Instead, at its onset, in men and women alike, certain swellings would develop in the groin or under the armpits, some of which would grow like an ordinary apple and others like an egg, some large and some smaller (6).

The plague affects the body by mimicking organic growth with its "swellings," which "would develop in the groin" and "grow like an ordinary apple" or an "egg." It is as if, situated in the groin, the plague takes over the reproductive mechanism of living beings, reproducing a lethal mimicry of life, and not just any life, but "an ordinary apple" or "an egg." The English word "buboes" — from which comes the name "bubonic plague" — derives from the Greek word for "groin." As with cancer or with viruses more generally, the mechanism of reproduction that normally assures the production and survival of living beings comes to signify their death.

"Against these maladies," Boccaccio continues, "no remedy was possible" whether due to the disease itself or to the lack of knowledge about it. The result was that "not only were very few people cured, but in almost every case death occurred within three days after the appearance of the signs we have described" (6).

But the plague does not just strike individuals in isolation from one another. It is no ordinary illness because it strikes people collectively. This raises the question of transmission. Although Boccaccio stresses that direct contact is responsible, he also invokes an image that suggests that contact alone is not enough to account for the spread of the plague: "Just as a fire will catch dry or oily materials when they are placed in close proximity [quando molto vi sono avvicinate]" (37).

In other words, vulnerability to the plague is not simply a factor of proximity or contact, since there are some persons, like "dry or oily materials," who are more disposed than others to catch fire or become infected. The idea here seems to be that susceptibility to the plague depends also on circumstances that are not easily identified. This conforms with the reality of the time: the plague was spread largely by fleas that in turn carried the bacillus from rats or from sick persons. But these fleas were often not easily visible. This raises the question of the transmission of the plague and to what extent it can be observed. There is a double problem here: what is visible is difficult to describe, and what is invisible is even more difficult to believe. This is how Boccaccio describes the situation:

What I have to tell is incredible, and if I and many others had not seen these things with our own eyes, I would scarcely dare to believe them, let alone write them down (7).

According to recent scholarship, it is highly unlikely the Boccaccio himself witnessed "these things" with his "own eyes," and it is certain that he relies on the eyes — and above all the written accounts — of others in order to compose what looks like a firsthand description of the plague.[4] This is a tendency that will also mark almost all accounts of the plague, just as it distinguishes the storyteller, according to Walter Benjamin, from the modern author as sole proprietor of his work. In Benjamin's view, the storyteller does not so much invent his stories as adapt them from previous stories, changing them in the process. As we will see, Boccaccio writes that this is what he has done. But the plague poses another problem: being a collective phenomenon, it is impossible for any one narrator to have witnessed it all, much less survived it. To recount the plague requires, therefore, relying not just on one's own eyes but also on the accounts of others. However, given how the effects of the plague defy the imagination, the authenticity of its reporting must again appeal to eyewitness accounts, and ultimately to the narrator or author's "own eyes." But in regard to the plague, the two tendencies converge, since the reliance on other accounts, the retelling of stories, goes together with the necessity to assume the first-person perspective of a singular eyewitness in order to be believable.

This tendency doubtless reflects the fact that the fury of the plague, although it strikes collectively, strikes at and through the lives of individuals. The "preexisting condition" that the plague needs to exist, much less to thrive — just as the virus needs a host — is the mortality and vulnerability of singular living beings. But these need not be exclusively human, as Boccaccio makes clear:

The plague that I have been describing was so contagious as it spread that it did not merely pass from one human to another, but we frequently saw something much more incredible, namely that when an animal of some species

78

other than our own touched something belonging to an individual who had been stricken by the disease or had died of it, that animal not only got infected but was killed almost instantly. With my own eyes, as I have just said, I witnessed such a thing on many occasions (7).

Boccaccio here speaks both in the first person ("with my own eyes, as I have said") and for the human species ("we frequently saw something much more incredible"), since the unbelievable event that he is describing concerns not just humans but animals in general. The plague strikes all living beings, no matter what their group or species. And it strikes them in a way that distinguishes the plague (and pandemics) from other catastrophes, by pitting life against itself, the living against the living, turning the mechanisms of vital reproduction against the survival of singular living beings.

On the one hand then, there is the need to have firsthand testimony, eyewitnesses, precisely because the plague produces such unbelievably catastrophic effects. On the other hand, the tendency of most of those subjected to the plague is to run away, to put distance between themselves and those it afflicts. This also has implications for the possibility of recounting the plague, which of course is what Boccaccio himself is doing here at the beginning of the Decameron:

> Those things and many others like them, or even worse, caused all sorts of fears and fantasies in those who remained alive, almost all of whom took one utterly cruel precaution, namely, to avoid the sick and their belongings, fleeing far away from them, for in doing so they all thought they could preserve their own health (7).

This tendency to flee the plague foreshadows what the protagonists in the *Decameron* will then decide to do: leave Florence, and establish their community somewhere outside in order to live and tell their stories without being in constant fear of contamination. But it also recalls the problematic position of the narrator who decides to report on the plague. As already noted, narrators of the plague almost always have to insist on a certain proximity to it, often a direct experience, in order to be believable. But at the same time, they have to explain how they could have survived it in order to recount it. Boccaccio states that he lived through the plague when it is probable that, like his storytellers, he was not in Florence at the time. But in describing the ravages it produced, he acknowledges both that he was close enough to know about it and far enough away to survive in order to recount it. Moreover, as a writer and not just a storyteller, Boccaccio commits himself to a medium that will survive him, just as he has survived the plague.

In placing the plague at the beginning and end of his stories, Boccaccio implicitly acknowledges that the stories he is writing down share something in common with the plague, namely, mortality. The stories may survive, if they succeed in being transmitted, that is, in being read. But they are no more eternal than the victims of the plague. And how they will survive depends not so much on the intentions of the author as upon the responses of the readers. This, too, they share in common with the plague. What plagues do is demonstrate that the mortality of individuals, as of societies and groups, is not something that can be fully controlled through calculation (although it can be influenced by it, as we will see when we discuss Defoe's *Journal*). The plague demonstrates the *limitations* — but by no means the *uselessness* — of all efforts to shape the future through planning and calculation, and ultimately to overcome the contingency of time. This is why all institutions that have justified their existence through the promise of such future security can be profoundly shaken to the extent that they reveal themselves to be incapable of protecting from the plague.

This is what Boccaccio describes as taking place in Florence. Once the future has been rendered totally uncertain and humans are confronted with their vulnerability and mortality, the result is not only that their respect for existing institutions and laws is shattered, but that the values that legitimated these laws and institutions are equally undermined. As Boccaccio puts it:

> In the midst of so much affliction and misery in our city, respect for the reverend authority of the laws, both divine and human, had declined to the vanishing point. . . . Thus people felt free to behave however they liked" (8).

This "freedom" produces a variety of responses — prudence, flight, resignation, hedonism — but what is common to all is the growing sense of isolation, which destroys even the most immediate familial ties:

> The plague had put such fear into the hearts of men and women that brothers abandoned their brothers, uncles their nephews, sisters their brothers and very often wives their husbands.[5] ... Fathers and mothers refused to tend to their children ... treating them as if they belonged to someone else (8).

Familial bonds are thus dissolved, and social constraints abandoned. But if fear weakens moral restraints, it also lays the groundwork for a different attitude toward eroticism among the survivors:

> There arose a practice hardly ever heard of before, whereby when a woman fell ill, no matter how attractive or beautiful or noble, she did not object to having a man as one of her attendants, whether he was young or not. Indeed, if her infirmity made it necessary, she experienced no more shame[6] in showing him every part of her body than she would have felt with a woman, which was the reason why these women who were cured were perhaps less chaste in the period that followed (9).

Since this is one of the very few references to "the period that followed" the plague — a period that the *Decameron* must presuppose if it is to be read — it is all the more significant that it suggests a more lasting weakening of religious and moral restraints upon erotic desires, which becomes one of the recurrent motifs of the stories in the *Decameron*. Another such motif is the resolutely egoistic nature of such desires, and this, too, is made all the more evident by the response to the plague.

Fear and flight thus dominate the reaction to the implacable plague. But although the *Decameron* itself will be the result of these impulses, Boccaccio takes pains to insist that flight from the city is anything but a reliable solution to the threat:

> But rather than go on recalling in elaborate detail all the miseries we experienced in the city, let me just add that the baleful wind blowing through it in no way spared the surrounding countryside. The fortified towns there fared just

like the city, though on a smaller scale, and in the scattered villages and farms the poor, wretched peasants and their families died at all hours of the day and night. Without the aid of doctors or help from servants, they would expire along the roads . . . and in their homes, dying more like animals than human beings. They, too, became as apathetic in their ways as the city dwellers were, neglecting their property (10).

In short, the somber frame that sets the scene for the *Decameron* sets it in a way that opens the question of just how the storytelling that will fill its pages relates to the plague that is both its starting point and — let us not forget — its end. For at the end of the ten days and one hundred tales, the participants return to a Florence that is still entirely in the grip of the deadly pestilence. The escape from its ravages is thus, as has often been observed, anything but a utopian project — it does not present an *alternative* to the plague, but a *response* to it. To discuss fully what sort of a response it is, would require an examination of the totality of the one hundred stories that compose it, something that is beyond what can be attempted here. Instead, I will have to limit my discussion here to just two of the many stories in order to advance a few hypotheses concerning not so much the *Decameron* per se, as the relation it stages between the plague and storytelling. As I have indicated, if there is a relation between the plague and storytelling in the *Decameron*, it is never direct. The stories do not recount the plague as such, but rather its social and cultural "preconditions."

The two stories discussed here are first, the story of Lisabetta, told on the fourth day, dedicated to lovers "who came to an unhappy end" (116). This is in accordance with the rules established by the group of storytellers at the outset, namely, that each day's stories should be organized around a common theme. The second story is the final story in the whole series, the tenth story told at the end of the tenth day. The stories on this last day are to be dedicated to the motif of magnanimity (*magnificenzia*), but as we shall see, this final story presents the theme in a very unexpected light.

But first to Lisabetta. This short tale is the one that is most commonly associated with the plague, because it recounts not just a death but the physical disintegration of a corpse reminiscent of the lethal effects of the plague. Here is a short summary of the plot: Lisabetta, a young "beautiful and well mannered" woman, living in Messina with her brothers, falls in love with Lorenzo, an employee in her family's business. Because of the social gap that separates the two lovers, they keep their relationship secret. But in time it is discovered, and Lisabetta's brothers, fearing a scandal, secretly murder Lorenzo and hide his body. After she has puzzled for a while over Lorenzo's absence, his ghost appears before Lisabetta and informs her about his murder and also where his corpse can be found. She visits the site, finds the body, and first tries to exhume it and take it home with her. But when she is unable to accomplish this, she decides instead to cut off the head to keep as a memorial. She takes the head home, hides it in a pot full of basil, and waters it with her tears each day. Noticing her strange behavior, her brothers become suspicious, discover the head in the pot, take it away, and bury it secretly. They then leave the town of Messina and move to Naples. When she discovers that the head is missing, Lisabetta weeps herself to death, "thus bringing her ill-fated love to its end" (138).

However, the story does not quite end with Lisabetta's death; it ends with a kind of afterword, a postface of sorts, which is difficult to designate as belonging to the tale or merely an appendix:

> In the course of time, however, people did learn the truth about the affair, and one of them composed the song that we still sing today, i.e. [cioè: in English, "that is to say"]: Who was that wicked Christian man / Who stole my pot of herbs from me etc. (139).

Walter Benjamin, you may remember, insists that no story ends without inviting its listeners to ask, "And what happened next?" The sad story of Lisabetta tells us what happened next. First, the truth about Lorenzo's death and about her own becomes known. And then, this knowledge is memorialized in a song — "a song that we still sing today." If you search on the internet for Lisabetta, you will find that "today" includes not just the time of Boccaccio but our time as well. Articles, stories, and songs continue to be composed concerning Lisabetta. This is surely related to another point Benjamin makes in his essay on the storyteller. True storytellers, like medieval chroniclers and certain historians — Benjamin gives an example from Herodotus — do not try to conclude their accounts by giving them a definitive meaning. The meaning is left open, and thus the story invites continued and active participation of its readers and listeners. This is even more so in Boccaccio's text since we are given not the song itself but only its first two lines, its *capo* (head), one could say. In musical discourse, *da capo* is the Italian term that indicates that one should return to the beginning, to "the head" as it were.

But it is not just that we are only given the first two lines, the *capo*, of the lament that is significant. It is the way we are given this that adds to its power, albeit in a very strange way. This strange non-end or after-life of the story is presented through a kind of shorthand abbreviation: *cioè*, meaning "that is (to say)," introducing the song's beginning, which does not so much conclude as stop with another shorthand abbreviation, *ecc.* The word that is here abbreviated, "et cetera," derives from the Latin, *caeterum,* meaning "the rest." In a certain sense, then, one can say that Lisabetta's story, somewhat like the plague itself, does not stop with the death of the individual. Indeed, one could argue that it begins there, or rather, starts all over, just as the beginning and end of plagues and pandemics are never entirely clear. And this is perhaps because they have no absolute beginning. Derrida begins an essay entitled "Et cetera" by declaring that "In the beginning, there was the 'et'. . . ."[7] Just as all stories, according to Benjamin, have no absolute beginning because they are taken from other stories that they adapt and transform, and no absolute end, because they are then themselves taken up and modified, so too with the story of Lisabetta — and perhaps also with plagues. But there is always a gap between the repetitive process in which storytelling is inscribed and the singular stories themselves. It is this gap that is both underscored and held open by the shorthand formulae, *cioé* and *ecc.* They preserve the tension that separates and links the fate of singular living beings, who are mortal and finite, to their indefinite repetition in story and song.

By insisting that Lisabetta's story gives rise to a lament, "which we still sing today," Boccaccio insists that the "once upon a time" of the story is not enclosed in a fictional past cut off from the present of its future readers. But although the song opens the story to the future, it does not do this abstractly or absolutely. Even if it is not present in its totality, the opening of the song still points us in a specific direction: "Who was the bad Christian/who stole my vase etc." (*Quale esso fu lo malo cristiano/che mi furò la grasta, et cetera*).

The "et cetera" both devalues the rest of the lyrics and at the same time revalorizes them by opening up a possibly indefinite repetition. It suggests on the one hand that what is not explicitly included in the citation will only be more of the same. But it also leaves open the possibility that this "same" will be significantly different and new. It makes us curious to know "what comes next." For the sentence that precedes the "et cetera" invites readers to reflect on just what, exactly, makes a Christian into a "bad Christian." In this particular case, but also in many others recounted in the *Decameron*, the question is raised of the relation between a certain Christian code of ethics, based on sin and penance, and the no less Christian emphasis on the saving power of love.

What are the forces that can make earthly love between two persons the object of such murderous violence, as well as of adulation (the tradition of courtly love is very much in the background of the *Decameron*)? Whatever the response will be, it will bear on the "preexisting conditions" to which the plague, like the stories told here, does not simply intervene but responds.

As already indicated, only an exhaustive reading of the *Decameron* in its entirety could hope to give a satisfactory response to this question. In the absence of such a reading, I will simply offer a hypothesis based on a reading of the second story I want to discuss, the one that concludes the whole cycle and to which I now turn.

This story is introduced by Dioneo, who, as Wayne Rebhorn has remarked, "distinguishes himself throughout . . . as the most irreverent and subversive of the storytellers" (xxx). Dioneo has from the start insisted that he be allowed to tell stories in his own way, even if this way diverges somewhat from the agreed-upon motif, and he is granted this exceptional status in part due to his young age. Here, too, at the very end of the ten days, he does not disappoint, since he begins by challenging the very idea of "magnanimity" that has organized the last day's tales:

> I want to tell you about a Marquis whose behavior was not an example of magnanimity, but of insane bestiality. And even though things turned out well in the end, I would not recommend that you follow his lead (331).

We recall again Benjamin's insistence on the pragmatic dimension of storytelling, which seeks to respond to a situation of distress, of total lack of orientation, of *Ratlosigkeit,* by giving counsel. Just what counsel one might glean from Dioneo's final story will be discussed after the following passage from Boccaccio's initial plot summary:

> Induced by the entreaties of his vassals to take a wife, the Marquis of Saluzzo, wanting to choose one his own way, selects the daughter of a peasant. After he has had two children with her, he makes it look to her as though they have been put to death. Later on, pretending to have grown weary of her, he claims he has married another woman and arranges to have his own daughter brought home as though she were his bride. Meanwhile, having turned his wife out of doors wearing nothing but her shift, on finding that she has borne everything with patience, however, he takes her back home again, dearer to him than ever, shows her their grown-up children and honors her as Marchioness and causes everyone else to do so as well. (331)

This story is one of the relatively few in the *Decameron* for which scholars have been unable to find any clear antecedent. Boccaccio is, again, like Benjamin's storytellers, for the most part repeating and reworking previous stories, thus confirming his profound relationship to a tradition that is in a process of radical change at the time he is writing. As mentioned previously, this change involves a shift from the transcendent, religious perspective that dominated most of the European Middle Ages, to a more "secular," earthly-bound sense of existence. Nevertheless, the two elements, transcendence and immanence, remain profoundly related, albeit in a very complex and conflictual manner, as this story will suggest. One thing that is changing is the status of hierarchy. Previously based on the belief that all worldly life derives from a Supreme Being that is all-powerful, universal, and exclusive (an initial model that was significantly altered into the holy family of Father, Son, and Holy Ghost but which retained its hierarchical structure), the problem becomes how to reconcile this monotheological conception of authority with social distinctions that no longer can be justified in terms of a divine hierarchy. This situation can be seen in the way Dioneo introduces his story. Magnanimity will no longer be examined by looking at earthly sovereigns whose generosity could be expected to reflect the absolute power of a divine Creator. Rather, it will be examined in the context of social differences that cannot be legitimated easily as reflecting the divine right of kings:

> My gentle ladies, the way I see it, we have given this entire day over to kings and sultans and people of that ilk, and therefore, lest I stray too far from the path you are on, I want to tell you about a Marquis. (331)

Dioneo thus begins by reassuring his listeners that he will not "stray too far from your path" (*troppo da voi non mi scosti*) — a path that associates magnanimity with sovereign figures: "kings, sultans and people of that ilk" (*così fatte gente*) — and so he chooses to tell the story of a Marquis, a nobleman to be sure, but not an absolute ruler. Nevertheless, this nobleman behaves like the most sovereign of sovereigns, at least in his relation toward his faithful wife, a narrative thread that makes up the substance of the story. His wife's name is Griselda, a name that recalls the Trojan figure of Criseida who betrays her (faithful) husband, Troilus, in Boccaccio's romance, *Il Filostrato*.[8] Boccaccio's use of the name, Griselda, is a good example of what I have been calling "friction." What is important is not so much that the name refers to a purely literary figure, and can therefore be thought of as fictional, but rather that the figure to which the name refers represents the exact opposite of what she will turn out to be: betrayal as opposed to absolute loyalty, or perhaps better, obedience. The name Griselda thus has a double significance. It echoes the sound of another figure whose characteristics of faithlessness it denies. But it remains connected to that figure even through the denial, and above all through the trials to which she is submitted by her husband, the Marquis. In the background of this very earthly story stands, however, another antecedent, this time not literary but theological. The Marquis behaves toward his wife in a manner that inevitably recalls the treatment of Job by the Lord with the same purpose, namely, to test her fidelity and obedience. Since this turns out to be total, she is rewarded at the end, as is Job. But whereas Job permits himself to entertain some doubts about the treatment he is receiving, Griselda does not. And she does not because of two reasons: one social, the other ethical. What is most obvious, and to most modern minds quite repugnant, is her sense of class hierarchy. As a poor servant girl elevated through marriage to a rich nobleman, she shows herself ready to accept absolutely whatever he decides to impose upon her, including the murder of their children and total destitution.

Griselda, like Job, accepts all of these acts of the Marquis. Although her husband is not God, she argues that all of her life with him, including their two children, is the result of a gift — the gift he has given her in marrying her. The famous phrase pronounced by Job, although never quoted in the story, is very much present in her reasoning:

> Naked I came from my mother's womb, and naked shall I return there. The Lord giveth and the Lord taketh away. (Job 1:21)

But what of this analogy between Job and Griselda, between the Lord, Creator of Life, and the Marquis, father of her two children? Dioneo, who tells the story, announces at the outset that it will not be so much about magnanimity as about a case of "insane bestiality" (*una matta bestialità*). What is already problematic in the behavior of an absolute Creator-God — Why, after all, should He have the need to put His creature to the test of loyalty? — becomes madness when it governs the behavior of a Marquis, who thereby confuses his elevated social position with a divine right. But Dioneo and the Marquis both share a certain characteristic, which is the desire to behave in a way that is not prescribed by general laws. Dioneo, as we have mentioned, insists on telling his stories in his own way, even if this diverges from the commonly agreed theme; and the Marquis insists, at the outset of the story, on being able to choose his wife in a way he pleases rather than in a way that would conform to social expectation. In both cases, then, we have the insistence on the irreducible right of singular human beings to challenge the generalities of the society in which they live. However, whereas Dioneo does this in a process of storytelling, the Marquis both uses the power that his social position confers upon him and at the same time does so in a way that reflects the desire to be an absolute ruler, the object of unlimited loyalty. This is precisely the point where the experience of what I call "singularity" and the ambition of "individuality" converge and separate. They converge in the Marquis, and they separate in Dioneo because the singular is not the individual, but rather highly dividual: it is what does not fit in, ultimately not even with itself.

The desire of the individual for absolute loyalty and absolute power is precisely what the plague calls into question. For the plague shows that no matter how great the power of individuals may be, they remain mortal and vulnerable.

Perhaps this is one reason why Boccaccio is more comfortable in addressing his stories to women than to men. For women, by their place and role accorded them in the society he wrote, have an experience of vulnerability that men often refuse to accept. Women in fourteenth-century Italy, as Boccaccio emphasizes in his preface, are largely cut off from action and decision-making. This is not the case with the women who tell stories and preside over the group of storytellers; in everyday life, they are shut up in their rooms and homes long before the plague arrives to force people to confine themselves. But in their confinement, they also have access to feelings and passions that, paradoxically, men, who can live out their desires more easily, cannot experience. In the *Decameron*, the seven women and three men escape the confinement of the plague in order to confine themselves in a different way. The framed narratives of the *Decameron* repeat and transform this particular sort of confinement in a way that I have been calling "frictional" rather than simply "fictional." Frictions do not liberate from the confinements of reality but transform them. They incorporate elements that designate existing entities, persons, things, and places, but transpose them into a realm where their significance can be altered and developed without being crushed by the weight of reality.

Thus, it is not only narcissistic irony when Boccaccio, in his conclusion to the stories, writes that "although I am a man of some substance . . . let me assure you that I am not heavy. In fact, I am so light that I float on the surface of the water" (344). This is a response to moralistic critiques of his language and thought: "It is perfectly clear that these stories were not told in a church," and it is equally clear that, "like everything else, these stories, such as they are, may be harmful or helpful, depending on the listener" (342). The storytellers meet in the church of Santa Maria Novella, and they flee it in order to organize themselves around a different sort of "novella," which is Boccaccio's Italian word for stories: new and old at the same time.

With his novella, Boccaccio, like Benjamin's storyteller, offers to give counsel and perhaps even consolation. But he knows that the particular counsel the stories will give will depend on how they are read and listened to:

> All things, in themselves, are good for some purpose, but if they are wrongly
> used, they will cause a great deal of harm. And I say the same thing about my

tales. Anyone who wishes to extract some wicked counsel from them or to come up with some wicked plan will not be prevented from doing so by the tales themselves. . . . But anyone seeking profit and utility in them will not be prevented from finding it either (343).

And this is why it is not a merely conventional disclaimer when Boccaccio insists that he is not the author of the tales but the scribe, the writer, and that therefore he could not pick and choose which stories to include and which to omit because they might cause offense:

> Indeed, I had an obligation to write down what was actually said. . . . But even if people assumed that I was not just the writer but the inventor of the stories — which I was not — then I would still reply that I am not ashamed of them . . . because there is no craftsman other than God who has made everything perfect and complete (343).

Unlike the theological notion of the author, which continues to console and distract readers even today by taking them "off the hook" and allowing them to look for an original intentional meaning informing texts, the writer, like the storyteller, knows that s/he is neither the origin nor the end of the text. Benjamin's observation is no less relevant to Boccaccio than to Leskov:

> The storyteller takes what he tells from experience — his own or that reported by others. And he in turn makes it the experience of those who are listening to his tale.[9]

Like the storyteller, Martin Luther uses his own experience to give advice. Unlike Boccaccio's figures, however, he will not seek to flee the plague by means of literary frictions but will rather stand his ground in an appeal to faith. In the role of letter writer, he discusses the obligation of the individual to community and to God in a time of plague.

The Lutheran Response: The Neighbor (Luther, "Should a Christian Flee the Plague?")

Walter Benjamin emphasizes that storytelling is often a response to a demand for "counsel" or "advice" — *Rat*. But it must be remembered that storytelling is not the only possible way in which advice can be offered. From August to November 1525, the plague ravaged the German city of Breslau. Whoever could, fled the city, while the municipal government sought to control the outbreak "through strict measures, in particular against the sick who thoughtlessly infected the healthy."[1] In view of the flight from the city, which included many religious officers of all faiths, Pastor Johannes Hess, representing a group of Evangelical (Lutheran) theologians and pastors, sent a letter to Martin Luther asking for his advice in this moment of great and imminent danger. The specific question that Pastor Hess addressed to Luther — "Whether it is seemly for a Christian to flee the general dying?" (*Ob es einem Christenmenschen gezieme, vor dem allgemeinen Sterben zu fliehen?*) — remained without an answer for almost two years, the time it took for the plague to finally arrive in Wittenberg, where Luther was living (225). Two years after receiving no reply from Luther, Pastor Hess renewed his request, and this time Luther set about composing a response. The time of his writing would coincide with the time the plague was active in Wittenberg, from July to November of 1527. Given the arrival of the plague, Luther had a first-hand occasion to give not just a theological but a practical response to the question of Pastor Hess. In August of 1527, the ruler of Wittenberg, Kurfürst Johann, ordered all members of the university (to which Luther also belonged) to migrate to Jena in order to avoid the plague. Most did so and stayed there until the following April, long after the plague had receded. Luther refused to leave, for reasons that he then detailed in his fifteen-page letter to Pastor Hess. During the plague period, Luther continued to hold lectures, to preach, and to exercise other priestly functions, including administering rites to the victims of the disease.

Nevertheless, his response to the question posed by Pastor Hess is, despite the frequent violence of his style, not unequivocal. It is not a yes or no, but an "it depends." And anyone who has read some of Luther's writings will not be entirely surprised to discover on what this decision depends, namely, on *faith*. For in Luther's eyes, it is "faith" that "overcomes death" (121). If this is not the essence of the Christian message, it is surely one of its most powerful attractions, and one that Luther makes full use of. In a mock dialogue with the devil, whom Luther holds responsible for the suffering and the plague, he summarizes the situation as follows:

> No, you shall not have the last word! If Christ shed his blood for me and died for me, why should I not expose myself to some small dangers for his sake and disregard this feeble plague. If you can terrorize, Christ can strengthen me. If you can kill, Christ can give life (128).

The "last word" is not to be had either by the plague, instrument of the devil, or by death itself, for it only threatens "my weak flesh," whereas "Christ, with his precepts, his kindness, and all his encouragement" is "far more important in my spirit" (128). We see that we are in a very different world from that of Boccaccio, some two centuries earlier, or from that of Thucydides, some two thousand years previous. And this, notwithstanding the fact that the second "wave" was in some ways more lethal than the Black Plague itself, which claimed the lives of up to 50% of the population of Europe while ravaging Asia and North Africa as well. The difference between the two responses to the epidemic, that of Boccaccio and that of Luther, however, was related not so much to the objective lethality of the pestilence, but to the attitude of those whom it affected. Luther's letter is one example of this difference. As always, it exemplifies how the effects of any plague can never be separated from the "preexisting conditions" of the societies it impacts. Those conditions involve not just the structure of the societies affected but the cultural attitudes of the people living in them.

The plague arrived in Breslau and then Wittenberg almost exactly ten years after Luther had promulgated his Ninety-five Theses, thus instituting what was to become a historical schism in Western European Christianity. The arrival of the plague thus intervened at a moment of spiritual and political crisis, but also of religious reinvigoration and conflict. A key point at issue in this conflict is already named by Luther in the German title of his letter, although it is effaced in most English translations. Literally translated, the title of Luther's text reads, "Whether One May Flee from Death." In German, the word for plague, *Pest*, is not mentioned — only "death," or more precisely, "dying": *Ob Man vor dem Sterben fliehen möge*. What is named is not the plague as an objective entity, nor even "death," but rather dying, and this changes the situation somewhat. For dying is an inevitable part of living, even if it ultimately puts an end to life on earth by what is called "death." And as we have already seen, the relation of life and death stands at the heart of the Christian message and the Good News, which promises that death, as the result of sin, can be overcome by faith in the sacrifice of Christ and in the Scripture that recounts it. If the devil, as the personification of sin, "kills, Christ can give life." The emphasis here is on the "can" — for it applies only to those who have faith. This is why Luther at the beginning of his Letter articulates the Pastor's question in a way that distances it especially from the title given his letter in English. For it is no longer a question of "one" — should *one* flee the plague? — but rather of a "Christian human being" (*Christenmenschen*); and not whether s/he should flee the plague, but rather the general dying, the *allgemeinen Sterben*. In German, the word for "general" or "universal" here is *allgemein*, literally, common to or shared by all—by all living beings as singular beings.

But human beings are not just singular. Although the social changes taking place in European culture and politics at the time of the Reformation were destined to emphasize the singularity of persons, places, and political entities against the previously claimed universal authority of the Catholic Church, this did not imply relegating such individuals to total isolation, or to total self-sufficiency. Recent scholarship emphasizes that the period of the Reformation was one in which social life was being transformed in the direction of an ever-greater emphasis on the importance of local communities. Luther's emphasis in his Letter on the obligation of Christians toward their "neighbors" provides a theological correlative to what has been described as the general social tendency of the time toward "communalization."[2] Very early in the letter, Luther makes it clear that individuals have two complementary obligations, and the German word he uses to make this argument is theologically overdetermined: *Schuld*, debt and guilt. Human beings are indebted to their Creator and responsible for each other. For, as he quotes Paul, "No one lives by himself, no one dies by himself" (Rom. 14:7). The German word used by Luther to name the other to whom one is responsible is *der Nächste*, usually translated as "the neighbor." This translation is not simply wrong, but as is often the case with translations, it misses an important nuance of the German word. In German, one can distinguish between *der Nachbar*, which is the equivalent of the "neighbor," and *der Nächste*, which is more abstract because it is derived from *Nähe*, "closeness, proximity." It is the latter word that Luther uses in the letter. It encompasses the idea of neighbor qua *Nachbar*, but also transcends it.

The general principle that Luther invokes to respond to the question of whether a Christian has the right to flee the lethal dangers of the plague or not is thus related to his interpretation of one's obligation to one's "neighbor," both as one who shares a contiguous locality or genealogy — parents, family — and also as one who shares a similar set of beliefs. But this double determination is also revelatory of the ambiguous and indeed ambivalent character of this principle of proximity. For how can any "proximity" be defined without a fixed point of reference in relation to which closeness or remoteness can be determined? The appeal to "faith" here is not adequate, for it does not sufficiently localize the point of reference. Faith, yes, but in what exactly? Here, problems arise, as the following argument brought forward by Luther clearly indicates:

> If I see that [my neighbor] is hungry or thirsty, I cannot ignore him but must offer food and drink without considering the danger of this making me poor or diminished. For whoever will help and sustain others only insofar as it does not involve the possibility of harming his property or his body, will never help his neighbor [*Nächsten*], for there will always seem as though it involves an interruption, danger, harm, or loss. But of course no neighbor [*Nachbar*] can live next to another without risking his body, property, woman, and child, which is why he must risk with him the danger that a fire or other accident coming from his neighbor's house [*Nachbars Haus*] might ruin his body, property, woman, and child, and everything that he has (125–26).

Faith must be individualized, but in so doing it raises the question of how individuated human beings, as well as their localized institutions, relate to one another. Proximity, whether as the "nearest" (*Nächste*) or as the "neighbor" (*Nachbar*), emphasizes closeness but not absolute identity. The word *Nachbar*, as we have seen in the passage just quoted, is used when it is a question of the place where one lives, one's house, whereas *Nächste* designates a more abstract kind of "closeness" and commonality. In the gap that separates the two — spiritual closeness from spatial-temporal proximity, *Nächster* from *Nachbar* — hostility can easily arise, especially in situations of extreme scarcity or urgency. We have already seen in Thucydides's and Boccaccio's descriptions of the effects of the plague, how the most intimate and most traditional bonds, beginning but not ending with those of the family, dissolve before the fear of impending death. Luther's conception of faith in no way eliminates this possibility: "It takes more than a milk faith" (1 Cor. 3:2) not to flee from death, a prospect "that terrified almost all of the Saints and continues to do so" (120). What perhaps is new here is that the relation to God passes via the relation to individuals and to localized communities. These are composed of interdependent members, who, however, qua individuals are still separate from one another, especially in their relation to mortality. This is why, as already noted, Luther has to insist, quoting Saint Paul, that these individuals do not live alone nor die alone.

But the ability to see the end of one's earthly existence as not ultimate and irrevocable is precisely what measures the "strength" or power of one's faith; this distinguishes the stronger faith of adult Christians from the "milk faith" (*Milchglaube*) of the weaker and immature.

On the other hand, Luther acknowledges that individuation produces differences even "among Christians," of whom he admits that "many are weak and few are strong" (120) and hence that it is impossible to make the same demands of both groups. Indeed, precisely because of such differences, it is imperative that those who exercise priestly functions not abandon the others: "For when people are dying they need spiritual aid most of all," in order to "overcome death through faith" (121).

For Luther, then, strength and weakness of faith can be measured in part by the importance attached to earthly-corporeal existence as distinct from heavenly-spiritual afterlife. The plague is merely one instance of the dichotomy that for him marks the relation of the Christian to life and death. But the relativization of earthly life in relation to a spiritual afterlife does not imply abandonment or devalorization of the desire for individual self-preservation. The desire to preserve one's life, he declares, is "natural and implanted by God" (123), and its only limit is that it should not involve harming one's "neighbor" (123). For the life of the individual, Luther insists, is utterly dependent upon the lives of others, brought together in a community that is religious but also political, local and yet universal.

Thus, Luther's response to the question posed by Pastor Hess involves the basic relation of individuals to each other and to the communal institutions upon which their lives depend. If no harm is done to neighbors or the community, he asserts, Christians may flee the plague with a good conscience. Otherwise, they may not. They may also choose to stay to aid others and the community. The question of fleeing the plague thus for him depends on the specific circumstances that obtain and that relate individuals to each other and through each other to the local and universal community to which they belong.

In response to the arguments of those who would justify flight from death only when the danger comes from human persecution, as frequently occurs in the Bible, Luther demurs, asserting in an unforgettable phrase, that "death is death no matter from where it comes" (*Tod ist Tod, er komme, wodurch er komme*) (124/231). Death as the end of earthly life is thus asserted to have a significance that transcends its specific cause. In this sense, the plague can be seen as a special case of the more general situation of human beings as mortal. Hence, it can be referred to as *das Sterben* rather than as "the plague." But although Luther leaves open the possibility of the plague being a divine punishment for sins, he also acknowledges the legitimacy of living beings who seek to defend and protect their earthly existence, as long as it brings no harm to the community. Because of this importance attached to the community, Luther presents the plague not so much as a divine punishment to be accepted than as a weapon in the hands of the devil to be combatted. In this combat, the main weapon he urges is solidarity with one's neighbors:

> Now if a deadly epidemic strikes, we should stay where we are, make our preparation, and take courage in the fact that we are mutually bound together . . . so that we cannot desert one another or flee from one another (127).

Since "service to God is indeed service to our neighbor," Luther in the second half of his letter does not demur from making a series of very practical recommendations, of the sort that Defoe will elaborate on in his *Journal of the Plague Year*. One of these is to fight infection by removing the sick from contact with the healthy, while at the same time not abandoning them for "it is our duty to assist such a person and not forsake him in his plight" (133).

Thus, Luther's response treads a thin line between the universalization inseparable from the notion of a monotheistic deity, and the individuation and differentiation tied to the notion of the neighbor and the community. However, individuation tends for him to imply not just difference but opposition, which in turn means that there are both good and bad "neighbors." This alone can explain the power of the plague to grow through infection. These bad neighbors are not entirely human:

> I am of the opinion that all the epidemics, like any plague, are spread among the people by evil spirits who poison the air or exhale a pestilential breath that puts a deadly poison into the flesh (127).

The plague is thus personalized and rendered imaginable in the form of "evil spirits" who serve the devil and who are to be combatted. But on the other hand, once the ultimate cause of the infection has been determined, there is a continual path that leads to ever more earthly responses. For instance, the means through which these evil spirits work turns out to be quite physical and prosaic, involving poor hygiene:

> Our plague here in Wittenberg has been caused by nothing but filth. The air, thank God, is still clean and pure, but some few have been contaminated because of the laziness or recklessness of some (133).

Who exactly these people are who "because of laziness or recklessness" have contaminated the rest, Luther does not say. But he does give us some indications. First and already familiar, he points to those who neglect their duties to their neighbors. But there are many other examples of bad or derelict neighbors. For instance, there are those who:

disregard everything that might counteract death and the plague. They dis-
dain the use of medicines; they do not avoid places and persons infected by
the plague; but who lightheartedly make sport of it and wish to prove how
independent they are.... It is even more shameful to pay no heed to one's own
body and to fail to protect it against the plague as best he is able, and then to
infect and poison others who might have remained alive if he had taken care of
his body as he should have. He is thus responsible before God for his neighbor's
death and is a murderer many times over (131).

Luther's rhetoric shifts from that of identifying the plague as the
weapon of a demonic enemy to pointing out those members of the
community whom he characterizes as suicidal and as murderers. His
response to the lethal violence takes on an increasingly violent and
lethal tone. The devil turns out to be active within the community
itself; the enemy is within, close by, a kind of deadly neighbor. Only
an equally lethal counterforce can effectively oppose it:

Some ... keep it secret that they have the disease and go among others in the
belief that by contaminating and poisoning others they can rid themselves of
the plague and so recover.... What else are such people but assassins in our
town? Here and there an assassin will jab a knife through someone and no
one can find the culprit. So these folk infect a child here, a woman there, and
can never be caught. They go on laughing as though they had accomplished
something. Where this is the case it would be better to live among wild beasts
than with such murderers.... I appeal to the authorities to take charge and
turn them over to the help and advice not of physicians, but of Master Jack,
the hangman (132–33).

In short, there are neighbors who are "assassins in our town," "murderers" who are worse to live with than "wild beasts." The trajectory
that Luther runs through in his letter can thus be summarized as
follows: (1) There are strong and weak Christians, many more weak
than strong. They can flee the plague if their flight does not bring
harm to their neighbors and their community; (2) Faith can overcome death, but only insofar as it recognizes that one's obligation

to help one's neighbor is equivalent to loving God ("Service to God is indeed service to our neighbor"); (3) Individuals depend on each other and on the communal institutions they create, and in the face of the plague, they must remain faithful to the obligations this interdependence entails; (4) The plague is the work of "evil spirits" and ultimately of the devil, but it works through members of the community, neighbors living "in our town"; (5) These evil neighbors sin either through pride or through negligence, and in the worst case are instruments of the evil spirits in propagating the malady; (6) Those who deliberately seek to infect their neighbors deserve to be put to death. The plague is thus construed as the result of an intentional act, just as mortality is already explained in the Bible as the punishment for an intentional transgression. The response to the plague can only be equally intentional, even if "faith" cannot be attained simply by intention, but remains a gift of grace.

Luther's response to Pastor Hess thus makes use of two distinct, but also complementary arguments. First, one's behavior in the face of the plague — or rather, of "dying," *dem Sterben* — should be directed by the principle that love of neighbor is love of God, of Christ, and of the local community in which one lives. But second, the threat of death that the plague brings with it is only part of a greater threat, which is identified with "evil spirits," "the devil," and perhaps above all, with those who although living "in our town" subordinate love of neighbor to love of oneself. The plague that strikes the community must also produce solidarity with its victims, a solidarity that overcomes one's spontaneous feelings and fears:

> When anyone is overcome by horror and repugnance in the presence of a sick person, he should take courage and strength in the firm assurance that it is the devil who stirs up such abhorrence, fear, and loathing in his heart. He is such a bitter, knavish devil that he not only unceasingly tries to slay and kill, but also takes delight in making us deathly afraid, worried, and apprehensive so that we should regard dying as horrible and have no rest or peace (127).

The very power of the plague to destroy is evidence of its weakness and coming defeat. If "Satan is so furious," Luther writes toward the end of his letter, it is "perhaps (because) he feels that the day of Christ is at hand. That is why he raves so fiercely" (137). The correct response, Luther counters, is to be neither overly materialistic nor overly spiritual:

> Under the papacy Satan was simply "flesh".... Now he is nothing more than sheer "spirit" and Christ's flesh and word are no longer supposed to mean anything (137–38).

Luther's alternative to the excessive materialism of the Catholic Church and the excessive spiritualism of certain freethinkers is to insist on a certain convergence of "flesh and word" in Christ, and this convergence also determines his response to the plague. If it is the deliberate effect of a consciousness, Satan, who knows exactly what he is doing and why, the plague still requires agents, "assassins living in our town," in order to enact the Satanic attack upon the neighbors and the neighborhood. The only effective response to such bringers of death is death itself: the hangman. The plague must be combatted with its own means, directed against those who are guilty of spreading it.

Two hundred years earlier, during the outbreak of the Black Death in the fourteenth century, the Jewish population of Central Europe was often held responsible for the ravages of the plague. Writing in 1527, Luther still hoped to convert them, and therefore had not yet identified them as instruments of the devil. Ten years later, however, he would arrange to have them expelled from Saxony, Brandenburg, and many other German towns for reasons already suggested in his search for the causes of the plague. In his notorious tract from 1543, *On Jews and Their Lies*, he associated them with "filth" and "poison,"[3] the same characteristics to which he attributed to the plague.

In 1527, however, Luther, still cherished the hope of converting the Jews and was therefore more kindly disposed to them. He even mentions them in a significant and favorable context, again toward the end of his letter. One of the few practical recommendations he makes, in addition to advising Christians to go to Church and learn from the word of God "how to live and how to die," has to do with the material reality of death, namely, burials and cemeteries:

> It is very well known that the custom in antiquity, both among Jews and pagans, among saints and sinners, was to bury the dead outside the city. Those people were just as prudent as we claim to be ourselves. . . . My advice, there-fore, is to follow these examples and to bury the dead outside the town. Not only necessity but piety and decency should induce us to provide a public burial ground outside the town, that is, our town of Wittenberg. A cemetery ought to be a fine quiet place, removed from all other localities, to which one can go and reverently meditate upon death, the Last Judgment, the resurrec-tion, and say one's prayers. . . . If a graveyard were located at a quiet, remote spot where no one could make a path through it, it would be a spiritual, proper, and holy sight [heilig anzusehen] and could be arranged so that it would inspire devotion in those who go there. That would be my advice (136–37).

Das wäre mein Rat — that would be my advice. Luther, although not telling a story, is still giving advice, responding to the request for counsel coming to him from Breslau. He is not recounting the plague that visited Wittenberg at the time he was writing his letter. But in a way strangely reminiscent of Boccaccio's Decameron, he ends up advising his neighbors to relocate their cemetery, since as it stands, "not even the Turk would dishonor the place the way we do" (137). Luther advocated for a locus amœnus, "a remote spot where no one could make a path through it," and yet where all paths end.

Luther's appeal to faith as a way of withstanding the ravages of the plague is based on the existence of this locus amœnus as a place from which a certain observation — a sacred sight — can take place. It is the site from which the living can observe the dead, or rather, death, as long as it is death of the other. Luther even goes so far as to suggest that "it might even be arranged to have religious pictures and portraits painted on the walls" (137). Although Protestantism and Lutheranism in particular are associated with a rejection of repre-sentational imagery, when faced with the plague, Luther prefers to look it in the face — from a point that is both close enough to see it and far enough away to escape its ravages. This, perhaps, is why his "advice" takes the form not of storytelling, but of an exhortation that in turn depends on a *depiction*. The plague, for Luther, allows death to be depicted, not just as death, but as "the Last Judgment, [and] the resurrection" (137).

And if one asks, as Benjamin suggests of all stories, "What happens next," Luther's answer is clear: it is faith and prayer.

CHAPTER SIX

"Out of All Measures"

(Defoe, *A Journal of the Plague Year*)

Curiosity

In 1665, when the Great Plague of London began, Daniel Defoe was
five years old. Whatever he experienced of the plague was thus mediated by the accounts of others: his father, his uncle, and the many
documents he researched in preparing his docufiction. One question
that presents itself at the outset is not why, in 1722, he felt it necessary
to write on the plague — we know the answer and will come to it in
a moment — but rather why in so doing he felt obliged to construct
the elaborate fiction of a firsthand observer, named at the end only
by his initials: H. F., the initials of his uncle, Henry Foe. We know
that Defoe was very concerned about an imminent outbreak of the
plague, which had emerged on the European continent in 1719 and
which, one year later, killed between forty and sixty thousand people
in Marseille, in the same epidemic that Antonin Artaud would take
as his reference in his 1931 lecture, "The Theater and the Plague." But
why he chose to adopt the fiction of an eyewitness account is not
immediately obvious. For at the same time, Defoe used another, less
fictional mode to express his concern and to warn his countrymen
to prepare for the worst: one month before the *Journal* appeared in
print, he published a treatise, *Due Preparations for the Plague*. As the
title indicates, he details in the treatise a number of measures that he
feels should be instituted immediately to protect London and Britain

from yet another attack of the plague. For the plague of 1665 was by far not the first of its kind to occur, although it was one of the worst. Throughout the sixteenth and seventeenth century, London had been afflicted with plagues with disarming regularity: 1563, 1592, 1603, 1625, and 1636 saw outbreaks costing each time the lives of tens of thousands of persons. None, however, were on the scale of the 1665 plague, which would turn out to be the last major outbreak of its kind in Britain.

There was good reason, then, to be concerned when the plague reappeared in Europe in 1719. But this concern does not suffice to explain Defoe's choice to publish not just his treatise but the fictional *Journal* as well. To be sure, since his concern was to alert his countrymen and to move them to make preparations that he felt had not been sufficiently undertaken, the form of a docufiction would be appealing due to the greater impact it might have. Londoners in 1722 were no strangers to the plague, with over half a century separating them from the Great Plague of 1665, and this temporal proximity had perhaps instilled a sense of security that worked against allocating the money, energy, and resources required to properly prepare for a recurrence. More importantly, perhaps, Defoe had very recently had success with the publication of two novels, *Robinson Crusoe* (1719) and *Moll Flanders* (1722), and thus had discovered "fiction's power to reach people and spread his ideas."[1] In these novels, the story was told in the first person, a device that Defoe retained for his *Journal*, although the *Journal* purported to be a real, firsthand account of the Great Plague, and not a simple fiction.[2]

However, wherever it is a question of recounting the plague, the point of view of the observer is never indifferent. We have previously had occasion to discuss certain aspects of this in relation to Luther's notion of the neighbor and the neighborhood. The lethal ferocity of the plague both demands and defies first-person, eyewitness accounts. Both Thucydides and Boccaccio claim such proximity, probably fictitious in the case of Boccaccio and probably accurate in the case of Thucydides, who asserts that he survived being infected by the illness (which at the time, we should recall, was not yet as lethal as the bubonic plague would be).

A firsthand experience, or testimony of firsthand witnesses, is precious concerning the plague precisely because of the way it strikes individuals — often isolated out of fear of contagion, and yet always in relation to a larger collective — for instance, as residents of a certain area, whether neighborhood, city, or nation. At the same time, the plague itself resembles an individual in the way it is always localized and the way it moves. One of the striking things that emerges in Defoe's account is the dual rhythm of this movement. It moves slowly but strikes with deadly force. Defoe recounts meticulously how it first appears in the Netherlands before making its way to Britain, producing its first victims — "two Frenchmen . . . in Long Acre, or rather at the upper end of Drury Lane" (5). This ability to localize the plague and follow its movements will be one of the hallmarks of Defoe's account. The result, however, is what both invites and defies firsthand eyewitness observation. On the one hand, the plague moves and is situated as though it were something like a physical entity; but on the other hand, it itself remains invisible — only its lethal effects can be seen, noted, and enumerated. Numbers thus play a conspicuous role in Defoe's *Journal*, giving to the invisible character of the plague a more tangible quality. Its victims are counted, even if the count is soon challenged by the increasing number of victims.

Describing the location and trajectory of the plague is thus one way it is identified: it is retraced in spatial, temporal, and quantitative terms, by being localized and by its victims being counted. However, Defoe notes a strange hiatus in its emergence. Appearing in Britain at first in December of 1664, it seems then to subside for almost six months during the winter, only to reappear when the weather gets warmer (the opposite of what we have experienced with Covid-19). During what might be called its latency period — not a term used in the *Journal*, to be sure — the plague is described as progressing "very gradually and slowly," making its way from the "poor suburbs" in the west of London toward the center of the "City" (93). It moves like a living creature — which, as a bacteria-driven illness, in a sense it was — while at the same time remaining invisible. Quite precisely then, Defoe notes that it is "felt" rather than actually seen:

> It was felt at first in December, then again in February, then again in April, and always but a very little at a time; then it stopt until May, and even the last week in May, there was but 17 (93).

Even when the death toll would rise to "3000 a-Week," there were still people in the area who were hoping "that it would not be so violent among them" (93) and who therefore failed to make any preparations in the hope that "God would pass over and not visit as the rest was visited" (94).

Like the Athenians described by Pericles, such confidence in the ability to escape the force of future calamities resulted in an even more disastrous situation when the malady finally arrives:

> And this was the Reason, that when it came upon them they were more surprised, more unprovided and more at a Loss what to do than they were in other places (94).

Overconfidence and lack of preparation produced a panic, which once again recalls accounts of Thucydides and even more Boccaccio:

> This...took away all Compassion; self Preservation indeed appear'd here to be the first Law. For the Children ran away from their Parents, as they languished in the utmost Distress: And in some places...Parents did the like to their Children...Mothers, raving and distracted, killing their own Children; one was not far off from where I dwelt....for the Danger of immediate Death to ourselves, took away all Bowels of Love, all Concern for one another (95).

To be sure, Defoe adds, there were counterexamples, "Instances of immovable Affection, Pity and Duty, and some that came to my Knowledge; that is to say, by here-say: For I shall not take it upon me to vouch the Truth of the Particulars" (95).

Although one instance of mothers killing their children took place "not far off from where I dwelt," the narrator cannot vouch for

all the information he provides. His position is that both of a partici-
pant and of an observer. In both cases, he is limited by what can be
seen but his account is also trusted even if it concerns a phenomenon
that takes place largely behind closed doors and that, in any case, is
visible only in the terrible effects it produces, but never in itself.

This, then, is the central paradox of the *Journal*, which insists
that its account is largely based on firsthand experience, on what the
narrator or others saw, remembered, and wrote down. But from the
very beginning, it is made clear that the evidence of one's own eyes
has to be subject to the greatest skepticism. This starts with what
was widely considered to be a visible portent of the catastrophe to
come: "A blazing Star or Comet appear'd for several Months before
the Plague, as there did the Year after another, a little before the
Fire" (20). The Fire referred to here occurred the following year, in
1666, and destroyed 80% of the buildings in metropolitan London. In
both cases, the appearance of meteors was taken, especially retro-
spectively, as a sign of coming disaster. This phenomenon encouraged people to find similar visual events that could be interpreted as
announcing the coming plague. The narrator recalls the following
incident:

> One time before the Plague was begun . . . I think it was in March, seeing a
> Crowd of People in the Street, I join'd with them to satisfy my Curiosity,
> and found them all staring up into the Air, to see what a Woman told them
> appeared plain to her, which was an Angel cloth'd in white, with a fiery Sword
> in his Hand, waving it, or brandishing it over his Head. She described every
> part of the Figure to the Life; shew'd them the Motion, and the Form, and
> the poor People came into it so eagerly . . . YES, I see it all plainly, says one. . . .
> One saw his very Face. . . . One saw one thing, and one another. I look'd as
> earnestly as the rest, but . . . I could see nothing but a white Cloud. . . . The
> Woman endeavored to show it me but could not make me confess, that I saw
> it. . . . She turned from me, call'd me prophane Fellow, and a Scoffer; told
> me that it was a time of God's Anger . . . and that Despisers, such as I, should
> wander and perish (23).

Despite his skepticism about heavenly portents, the desire to see the plague and its effects drives what turns out to be one of the main motifs of the narrator, namely, his "Curiosity": it is "to satisfy my Curiosity" that he joins the crowd "staring up into the Air." And although in the end he sees not an Angel but "nothing but a white Cloud," his curiosity continues to drive him to forsake the relative safety of his home to see what is happening outside, no matter what the risk:

> But tho' I confin'd my Family, I could not prevail upon my unsatisfy'd Curiosity to stay within entirely my self; and tho' I generally came frighted and terrified Home, yet I cou'd not restrain (68).

Although doubtless what the narrator (and Defoe) mean to say here is that his "unsatisfy'd Curiosity" did not permit him to do himself what he imposed on his family, namely, to stay indoors, "entirely." The formulation "to stay within entirely my self" can also be read as his saying that curiosity made it impossible for him to stay within the bounds of his self; curiosity drives him to forsake his secured place of residence in search of something that turns out to be as terrifying as it is invisible. What is especially frightening about plagues, and what distinguishes them from wars, with which they are often compared, is that they attack not from without but from within. This makes them much harder to observe, and also much more uncanny.

Two incidents dramatize this uncanniness. First, H. F. defies the curfew in force to go out at night to view the burial of the dead, which by city ordinance could only take place at night to avoid spreading panic. Curiosity drives him to see the burial pits:

> It was about the 10th of September, that my Curiosity led, or rather drove me to go and see this Pit again, when there had been near 400 People buried in it; and I was not content to see it in the Day-time, as I had done before, for then there would have been nothing to have been seen but the loose Earth, for all the Bodies that were thrown in, were immediately covered with Earth [so] I resolv'd to go in the Night and see some of them thrown in. . . . tho it is impossible to say any Thing that is able to give a true Idea of it to those who did not see it (53).

Gaining admission to the churchyard and driven, as he repeats, by "no apparent Call but my own Curiosity,"

> I stood, wavering for a good while . . . and then appear'd a Dead-Cart, as they call'd it, coming over the Streets so I could no longer resist my Desire of seeing it, and went in. There was no Body, as I could perceive at first, in the Church-Yard [except] the Fellow that drove the Cart . . . but when they came up to the Pit, they saw a Man go to and again, muffled up in a brown Cloak, and making Motions with his Hands, under his Cloak, as if he was in a great Agony; and the Buriers immediately gathered about him, supposing he was one of those poor delirious, or desperate Creatures, that used to pretend . . . to bury themselves; he said nothing as he walk'd about, but two or three times groaned very deeply, and loud, and sighed as he would break his Heart. . . . When the Buriers came up to him, they soon found he was neither a Person infected and desperate . . . or a Person distempered in Mind but one oppressed with a dreadful Weight of Grief . . . having his Wife and several of his Children, all in the Cart, that was just come in with him, and he followed in an Agony and excess of Sorrow. . . . But no sooner was the Cart turned round, and the Bodies shot into the Pit promiscuously, which was a Surprize to him . . . no sooner did he see the Sight, but he cry'd out aloud unable to contain himself. I could not hear what he said, but he went backward two or three Steps, and fell down in a swoon. . . . In a little while he came to himself. . . . He look'd into the Pit again, as he went away . . . yet nothing could be seen (54–55).

The contrast between what can be seen — for instance, bodies heaped up in the cart and then "shot promiscuously" into the burial pit — and what cannot — after earth is hastily thrown over the corpses — is little short of traumatic: "I was indeed shock'd with this Sight, it almost overwhelm'd me. . . . I went away with my Heart most afflicted and full of afflicting thoughts, such as I cannot describe" (55). We reach the limits of the visible and the describable with this scene, which takes us with the narrator into the "pits" — or rather to their edge.

The second scene that demonstrates the tension between the visible and the invisible in H. F.'s account of the plague is less vivid, perhaps, but certainly not less dramatic. It is also relatively short. H. F. recounts how on his walks,

> I had many dismal Scenes before my Eyes, as particularly of Persons falling dead in the Streets, terrible Shrieks and Skreekings of Women, who in their Agonies would throw open their Chamber windows and cry out in a dismal Surprising Manner. . . . Passing thro' Token-House-Yard in Lothbury, of a sudden a Casement violently opened just over my Head, and a Woman gave three frightful Skreetches, and then cry'd, Oh! Death, Death, Death! In a most inimitable Tone, and which struck me with Horror and a Chilness, in my very Blood. There was no Body to be seen in the whole Street, neither did any other Window open; for People had no Curiosity now in any Case; nor could any Body help one another, so I went on (68–9).

Where nothing can be seen, cries fill the air, even if no one is there to listen — no one, that is, except H. F., the narrator. The casement window "violently" opens "just over my Head." The scene could hardly be closer. And yet it can barely be communicated for what it expresses is as "inimitable" as the cry itself.

It is through sound that thus the true horror of the plague is expressed and communicated. These are not the sounds of death, which is silent, but rather of the dying:

> I wish I could repeat the very Sound of those Groans, and of those Exclamations that I heard from some poor dying Creatures, when in the Hight of their Agonies and Distress; and that I could make him that read this hear; as I imagine I now hear them, for the Sound seems still to Ring in my Ears. If I could but tell this Part, in such moving Accents as should alarm the very Soul of the Reader, I should rejoice that I recorded those Things, however short and imperfect. It pleased God that I was still spar'd, and very hearty and sound in Health (86–87).

Defoe's fictional narrator, "H. F.," will, of course, be "spar'd" and left safe "and sounds in Health" in order to be able to recount the plague. He has survived. But the "Sound" of the dying "seems still to Ring in my Ears." This sound that was never heard by Defoe directly, and that cannot be heard now when it is read in a text, resonates with a particular intensity precisely in the non-acoustical medium of written language: the medium of the *Journal* and of its recounting. It resonates because, like visual elements of a text, it allows readers to imagine and feel what they can neither see nor hear.

Recounting the Plague: Tallying Its Tale

Numbers are everywhere in Defoe's *Journal*. The approach of the plague is signaled by the increase in the number of burials in the Western suburbs (44). As it becomes clear that the plague "defied all Medicine" and that "the very Physicians" who sought to treat it were themselves "seized by it," it seems as if the only countermeasures that can be taken are the shutting up of victims in their homes — thus condemning the other residents to become victims of infection. Defoe will consistently criticize this practice and recommend that for the future, places be created where victims of the plague can be isolated without exposing the persons around them to a similar fate. The plague cannot be treated, and its confinement as practiced is difficult and can be counterproductive. One result is that all those who are able to, flee the city. This begins with the Royal Court itself, which only four years earlier had been restored to power, and which had already earned itself a reputation for corruption and irresponsibility. The Court fled to Oxford where it stayed until the plague had subsided. Not so with the municipal government, which Defoe's narrator lauds for its courage and for the measures it takes in trying to help the poor, who, then as now, were disproportionately subject to the violence of the disease and to its effects. At first, then, it is the wealthy who decide to leave London. H. F., the narrator, immediately translates this into numerical terms:

> It was thought that there were not less than 10000 Houses forsaken of the Inhabitants in the City and Suburbs. . . . This was besides the Numbers of Lodgers, and of particular Persons who were fled out of other Families; so that in all it was computed that about 200000 People were fled and gone in all (63).

But those who are less well-off do not have this luxury as an option. The poor, who are particularly hard hit by it, are also among "the most Venturous and Fearless of it" (75), H. F. notes. Showing "a Sort of brutal Courage," the poor take on the most hazardous tasks in order to survive, although often they did not. H. F. estimates that between August and October the plague "carried off thirty or forty thousand of these very People" (81), noting, with cruel pragmatism, that had they survived, they

> would certainly have been an unsufferable Burden, by their poverty, *that is to say*, the whole City could not have supported the Expence of them, or have provided Food for them; and they would in Time have been even driven to the Necessity of plundering either the City itself or the Country adjacent . . . which would first or last have put the whole Nation, as well as the City, into the utmost Terror and Confusion (82).

In other words, together with the city government's decisive but brutal actions of shutting up families and groups in their houses, the plague fulfilled a Malthusian function of allowing the collective — the city and the nation — to survive by killing many of its poorest residents. And immediately after this brutally pragmatic reckoning, H. F. "verifies" it by inserting the "Bills of Mortality" for the months of August and September, the statistics of which, however, he then goes on to correct

> so that the Gross of the People were carried off in these two Months; for as the whole Number which was brought in, to die of the Plague, was but 68590 here, is fifty thousand of them, within a Trifle, in two Months; I say 50000, because as there wants 295 in the Number above, so there wants two Days of two Months, in the Account of the Time (82).

H. F. thus provides his readers with a recounting of the Bills of Mortality, taking into account that "two Days of two Months" are missing "in the Account of the Time."

Thus, the statistics provided in official Bills of Mortality require a corrective recounting, since, as H. F. notes, the "Parish Clerks" who were doing the counting were not immune from the illness. On the contrary, he notes,

> for tho' these poor men ventured at all hazards, yet they were far from being exempt from the common Calamity, especially, if it be true, that the Parish of *Stepney* had within the Year, one hundred and sixteen Sextons, Grave-diggers, and their Assistants, that is to say, Bearers, Bell-men, and Drivers of Carts, for carrying off the dead Bodies.
>
> Indeed, the Work was not of a Nature to allow them Leisure, to take *an exact Tale* of the dead Bodies, which were all huddled together in the Dark into a Pit, which Pit, or Trench, no Man could come nigh, but at the utmost Peril (82–83; italics added).

"The Work was not of a Nature to allow them Leisure to take *an exact Tale* of the dead Bodies." "An exact Tale . . . ." The common use of this word in Defoe's time to signify not "story," but rather "tally," provides us with a useful reminder of the common etymological root of the two terms. Both *telling* and *tallying* have to do with organizing a temporal sequence of events: the one with words, the other with numbers. But the numbers here, which in a tally establish the possibility of a uniform numerical sequence that can claim to be beyond temporal change, ignore the fact that the "dead Bodies . . . huddled together in the Dark" are not simply equivalent entities to be so tallied. Each corpse marks the end of a singular life that remains incommensurable with all the others. And therein lies a tale. But this tale, if it is singular, is never self-contained. For contrary to the assertion of Saint Paul, quoted by Luther, to which we have referred in the previous chapter, if it is true that no one lives alone, it is not equally true that "no one dies alone."[3] Even surrounded by family and friends, there remains a difference between the one who dies and the others who survive. This complex relation of singularity and plurality, of self and others, cannot be reduced to a numerical list. The enumeration of the dead can no more grasp the singularity of each victim than the eye of the observer can penetrate the "Dark" of the pit into which the bodies are "shot" by the grave diggers. The abrupt movement of being "shot" or "thrown" — verbs that H. F. uses in describing the ways the corpses are buried — emphasizes this radical break and discontinuity that binds and separates the living from the dead.

There is a tension then, if not a contradiction, between the lethal devastation wrought by the plague and the ability to count — and to recount — its effects. H. F. returns to this toward the end of his *Journal*, which is written not just for posterity, as are all texts, but more specifically as both a warning to readers and as an argument urging them to prepare for a possible recurrence of the plague. As Luther before him, Defoe does not condemn those who fled before the plague — before "dying" to quote Luther's letter — but rather urges his readers to take the full measure of the danger:

> I recommend it to the Charity of all good People to look back, and reflect duly upon the Terrors of the Time; and whoever does so will see that it is not an ordinary strength that could support it, it was not like appearing in the Head of an Army, or charging a Body of Horse in the Field; but it was charging Death it self on his pale Horse; to stay was indeed to die . . . especially as things appear'd at the latter End of August (184).

Kleist's Robert Guiscard and his followers will make a similar and shattering discovery. The plague is no ordinary enemy, least of all in a military sense, despite the fact that as in a military conflict, it kills and maims in great number or that in the case of the Great Plague of London, it would subside almost as suddenly as it had come. No one could have known or anticipated, H. F. continues, that the devastating plague that was killing twenty thousand persons a week in late August and early September of 1665, would suddenly begin to abate, thus sparing London and Britain even greater devastation. As it subsides, the time of collecting information and summing up begins to arrive. For H. F., this means attempting to compile "a List" not just of all the victims, but more specifically of all "who thus died . . . in the way of their Duty" (184). But once again, he acknowledges that "it was impossible for a private man to come at a Certainty in the

Particulars." After enumerating a few of the officials who so perished, he confesses to having been forced to abandon the task:

> I could not carry my List on, for when the violent Rage of the Distemper in
> September came upon us, it drove us out of all Measures: Men did then no
> more die by Tale and by Number. . . . They died by Heaps, and were buried by
> Heaps, that is to say without Account (184–85).

The plague defies numerical counting both because of the extent
of its devastation — men did not die "by Tale and Number" but "by
Heaps" — but also because each one of the dead, swallowed up in the
uncountable "heap" of corpses, represents a life that was unique and
thus capable of being told, but not simply tallied. The plague thus
becomes, in the *Journal*, the tale of a tale in the different senses of that
word: a story that cannot be tallied, and a tally that cannot be told.
This is why the *Journal* will be filled not just with tallies, but with
tales reflecting uniquely singular experiences of uniquely singular
persons.

Strange Effects

As has been mentioned, Defoe writes his *Journal* in the hopes of alert-
ing his countrymen to a possible future danger: that of the plague
returning to London from the continent. This did not materialize
possibly because of the greater control of movement that the previous plague had allowed the government to develop. This was also the
case in France, where the absolute regime stationed a quarter of the
French army on the borders of Provence in order to keep the plague
from spreading from the south to the whole country. This strategy
of surveillance and confinement succeeded in France, and perhaps
in Britain as well. We will never know for sure. But Foucault's argument, in *Discipline and Punish,* that the plague served as a transition
from a society of confinement to one of total surveillance, can hardly
be denied.[4]

In an indirect way, this shift also concerns Defoe in writing his *Journal*. But to understand, one must recall the particular

circumstances in which it was composed. England had only very recently emerged from a civil war following the Protectorate of Oliver Cromwell, which restored the monarchy four years before the plague arrived. The general political climate was one of restoration . . . and of revenge. Together with the return of the monarch, the Church of England was imposing its authority on the whole country, not just against Catholics but also against other Protestant Dissenters, of which Defoe was one. This is the context in which H. F. describes how the ravages of the plague produced in the population what he calls a very "strange Effect":

> As I have mentioned how the People were brought into a Condition to despair of Life and abandon themselves, so this very Thing had a strange Effect among us . . . that is, it made them bold and venturous, they were no more shy of one another, or restrained within Doors, but went any where and every where, and began to converse. . . .
>
> As it brought the People in publick Company, so it was surprising how it brought them to crowd into the Churches, they inquir'd no more into who they sat near to or far from . . . but looking upon themselves all as so many dead Corpses, they came to the Churches without the least Caution . . . [showing] what a value people would all put upon the worship of God if they thought every Day they attended at the Church that it would be their Last. Nor was it without other strange Effects, for it took away all Manner of Prejudice . . . the People made no scruple of desiring such dissenters as had been a few Years before depriv'd of their Livings by virtue of the Act of Parliament call'd, The Act of Uniformity (139).

And H. F. draws a consequence from these "strange Effects" that goes far beyond the concern with the coming plague:

> Here we may observe . . . that a near View of Death would soon reconcile Men of good Principles one to another. . . . Another Plague Year would reconcile all these Differences, a close conversing with Death, or with Diseases that threaten. Death, would scum off the Gall from our Tempers, remove the Animosities among us, and bring us to see with differing Eyes, than those which we look'd on Things before (140).

For H. F., it is the proximity to death that becomes the basis of a new neighborliness, recalling Luther's emphasis on the neighbor. But in contrast to Luther, H. F. has no illusions about what happens when the immediate danger, the confrontation with mortality, recedes or is repressed:

> I mention this but historically. . . . I do not see that it is probable such a Dis-course would be either suitable or successful; the Breaches seem rather to widen, and tend to a widening farther, than to closing, and who am I that I should think myself able to influence either one Side or the other (140)?

What we are left with, then, far from the universal reconciliation of all mortals in the face of a common death, is the series of unforget-table singular incidents that spot the pages of Defoe's *Journal*. I will conclude by citing just one more of them, an "afflicting sight" that H. F. purports to have seen from his apartment window:

> But I must still speak of the Plague as in its height, raging even to Desolation, and the People under the most dreadful Consternation, even as I have said, to Despair. It is hardly credible to what Excesses the Passions of Men carry'd them in this Extremity of the Distemper. . . . What could affect a Man in his full Power of Reflection and what could make deeper Impressions on the Soul, than to see a Man almost Naked and got out of his House, or perhaps out of his Bed into the Street, come out of Harrow-Alley, a populous Conjunction or Collection of Alleys, Courts, and Passages, in the Butcher-row in Whitechap-pel? I say, What could be more Affecting, than to see this poor Man come out into the open Street, run Dancing and Singing, and making a thousand antick Gestures, with five or six Women and Children running after him, crying, and calling upon him, for the Lord's sake to come back, and entreating the help of others to bring him back, but all in vain, no Body daring to lay a Hand upon him, or to come near him (136–37).

No one lives alone, to be sure. But it is not just the plague that con-fronts us with the painful solitude of dying.

CHAPTER SEVEN

Tragedy as *Trauerspiel*

(Kleist, *The Tragedy of Robert Guiscard,*

Duke of the Normans)

Even More Extraordinary ("Noch ungeheurer")

On October 5, 1803, Heinrich von Kleist wrote in a letter to his sister, Ulrike:

> Heaven knows, my dearest Ulrike (and I will perish, if it isn't literally true), that I would gladly give a drop of blood from my heart for every letter of a missive [*für jeden Buchstabe eines Briefes*] that could begin by announcing, "My poem is finished." But, you know the proverb, whoever does more than he can (. . . .) It would be foolish, at the very least, if I continued to devote all my energy to a work that, I have finally convinced myself, is too difficult for me. I yield before one who is not yet there, and bow, a thousand years in advance, before his spirit. For in the sequence of human inventions the one I have thought up is certainly a step [*ein Glied*], and somewhere a monument [*ein Stein*] is growing for the one, who will be able to express it one day [*sie einst ausspricht*].[1]

Death is never very far from the thoughts of Heinrich von Kleist, and indeed, not just death, but suicide. "I will perish [*umkommen*]," he writes his sister, if the letter he is about to send her "is not literally [*buchstäblich*] true." And he assures her, that he "would gladly give a drop of blood for every letter of the missive" in which he could announce that "my poem is finished [*fertig*]." Thus, this letter begins with a double announcement, or promise, of death. The object of this promise is nothing other than a play he has tried, unsuccessfully, to write: *Robert Guiscard, Duke of the Normans.*

Less than a month after writing Ulrike, Kleist sends his half-sister another letter, which begins with an equally desolate announcement:

> My dear Ulrike, be my strong girl! What I have to write you can perhaps cost you your life, but I must, I must, I must go through with it (*es vollbringen*). In Paris I have read through my work, as far as it was finished, and rejected and burnt it: and now it is over. Heaven denies me fame, the greatest of earthly goods. (. . . .) Without your friendship, I cannot survive: I am going off to die [literally: I throw myself to death, *ich stürze mich in den Tod*]. Don't worry, sublime creature, I will die a beautiful death on the battlefield (R 39).

Thus, In a few sentences Kleist confirms the failure of his attempt to write what he had hoped to be the classically modern German tragedy and at the same time explains, in part at least, why he had chosen this particular historical person — Robert Guiscard — to be its central figure. If one is going to die, it might as well be "on the battlefield." And Guiscard, although largely forgotten today, was precisely known for his warrior prowess. In his letter, Kleist is referring to his intention to enlist in Napoleon's army and participate in the then planned invasion of England. This project was never realized, no more than the tragedy itself. But if Napoleon fascinated Kleist no less than did Guiscard, it was perhaps because both were self-made military and political conquerors. Kleist did not live to see the end of Napoleon on the field of Waterloo, but he did try to recount the end of Guiscard. However, it was not on the battlefield that the historical Robert perished, or even close to it. Kleist situates the dramatic action, or inaction, at the gates of Constantinople. But the historical Robert succumbed to the plague far from his goal, namely, off the Western coast of Greece. However, precisely this failure to accomplish his dream of conquering Constantinople was to make Guiscard the exemplary hero of the tragedy that Kleist hoped to write.

He tried and abandoned the project twice. The first time was in 1803, when, as we have just read, he burned his manuscripts relating to it. This was, however, not his last word, or attempt. Four years later, in October of 1807, he wrote a letter to the celebrated writer and critic, Christoph Martin Wieland, in whose house five years before he had recited from memory the first act of the unfinished play; at the time, Wieland encouraged the young author to finish the play, declaring it to be a work of genius. In his letter of 1807, Kleist assures Wieland that he finally is going to finish his play, and this in the near future (*In Kurzem*), which once again he will not succeed in doing. This is not simply because of writer's block, however. For in the years following his initial abandonment of the project, Kleist was very prolific. In his letter to Wieland, he announces that in addition to the fragment of this play, he also has finished manuscripts of three other works in hand: a "mourning play" (*Trauerspiel*), *Penthesilea*, a comedy (*Lustspiel*), *The Broken Jug*, and a novella (*Erzählung*), *The Marquise of O*. But once again he is unable to complete the play and instead publishes its first (and only) act in 1808. Many years after Kleist's death, Ludwig Tieck, declared it to be a "masterful beginning" of what, had it been completed, could have become the author's "most accomplished work" (R 80).[2]

Kleist himself provides us a possible hint of why the play was so difficult for him to complete. In another letter, also from 1808, he declares, of the play:

> The first work I want to present is Robert Guiscard, Duke of the Normans. The content [*Stoff*] is, as people say, even more extraordinary [*noch ungeheuerer*]. But in art what is always decisive is form, and everything that has a shape [*Gestalt*] is made for me [*meine Sache*] (R 44).

The content or material (*Stoff*) of the play is "even more immense," more uncanny, *noch ungeheurer*. Kleist uses the comparative here, "even more," to describe the thematic content of the play. But just what is he comparing this to? More than what? The only possible point of comparison mentioned explicitly in the sentence is the proper name and social title of its "hero": Robert Guiscard, Duke of the Normans. The *Stoff* then is "even more extraordinary" than the person named, who is, to be sure, extraordinary enough. What is "more" and greater than the individual is his destiny and its effects. The challenge then was to give a "form" or a "shape" not just to this already extraordinary figure, but to his fate and everything it implies, in other words, to his encounter with the plague. It is precisely this that Kleist could not accomplish. The question is why, and with what significance?

"Built for Posterity"

In 1797, a military historian in the service of the Saxony provincial government, Karl Wilhelm Ferdinand von Funck, published a biography of the Norman warrior, Robert Guiscard, who emigrated from Normandy to southern Italy in the eleventh century, established his rule there, and almost succeeded in conquering the Byzantine Empire. The biography was published in a literary monthly, *Die Horen*, founded and edited by Friedrich Schiller. This was a main source of inspiration for Kleist in composing his drama. Funck portrayed Guiscard as someone who strove to immortalize himself "through glorious deeds" (R 53). We can recall Kleist's letter to Ulrike in which he called fame "the greatest of earthly goods." Both Guiscard and Kleist failed to achieve their immediate goal: Kleist's aim being that of completing the tragedy; Guiscard's being the conquest of Constantinople and thus the establishment if not of a world empire at least of a transcontinental one. He had already achieved dominance in the southern half of the Italian peninsula, his sphere of influence stretching from Naples to Rome and including Sicily. Now he sought to extend this by conquering Constantinople, center of the Byzantine Empire, which, at the time, was very much on the decline, it should be noted — although this plays no role in the tragedy. After defeating Alexius in 1081, in a naval battle that destroyed the enemy's fleet, Guiscard had to return to Italy to quell revolts there and counter the threat of Henry IV of Germany taking Rome. He thus could not follow up his victory. Four years later, however, he would try again. After an initial victory at the end of 1084, he spent the rest of the winter of 1085 preparing for a direct invasion of Greece. He had to leave one of his two sons, Bohemund, who had fallen prey to a fever — probably the same one that would take the life of his father — to recover at home in Italy while he and his other son, Roger, spent the winter months preparing the invasion. But as his ships and cavalry made ready to move toward Greece, as Funck writes, the unexpected happened:

> With frightening rapidity there spread among the ships a contagious illness. The heat of the summer added to the ferocity of the deathly plague (*Seuche*), and among the victims was now the Duke. He was brought on land . . . but the same means that had saved the life of the young Bohemund remained without effect on the sixty-year-old Robert. His spouse could barely make it in time to hold him in her arms as he died (R 58).

Kleist's other main historical source was a multivolume history of Alexius written by one of his daughters, Anna Komnene, part of which had also been published in Schiller's journal, *Die Horen*. Anna makes it clear that Guiscard and his troop came nowhere near Constantinople but instead were immobilized by the plague off the Western coast of Greece, at the island of Cephelonia, where Guiscard died.

Guiscard's death marked the end of the ambition of conquering the Byzantine Empire. As a recent historian puts it:

> Robert's death brought an abrupt halt to what had been very much a personal expedition. . . . William of Apulia wrote of the fear which enveloped his troops once they knew of his death, and their hasty and panic-stricken embarkation. . . . The opportunity for a further, and most ambitious, conquest had been fleeting, and soon disappeared.[3]

What Graham Loud, in the passage just quoted, calls "very much a personal expedition," was conditioned by a historical situation in which established empires were declining and new ones slowly emerging. In this situation, precisely such "personal expeditions" became possible in a way they would not have been under more stable conditions. This is how Funck, Kleist's main source, describes the historical situation:

Out of the ruins of the Carolingian monarchy new empires were slowly emerging, but none had yet established themselves firmly; and as long as no defined civil order distributed the places in the state, it was up to each individual to seek his own, following the measure of his abilities or his desires. With pleasure one lingers over the monuments of personal greatness, which the yearbooks of those times have preserved for us. . . . But even more attractive is such contemplation when the work of a great man was not only a passing phenomenon, not only for the short period of his life, but rather is built for posterity. . . . Only the state of the Normans in lower Italy remains connected, despite the revolutions of seven centuries, with today's conditions in Europe, and the provinces of the Lombards, the Saracens, and the Greeks, which Robert Guiscard united under his scepter, constitutes even today the kingdom of Naples (R 53–54).

For a writer such as Kleist, concerned with acquiring that "greatest of earthly goods," fame, this portrayal of Robert Guiscard, whose work, as Funck describes it, was "built for posterity," could only appear as a model — an indeed all the more exemplary one given the unsettled political situation in which the German states found themselves around 1800. At the same time, what the story of Robert Guiscard seemed destined to demonstrate was not the achievement of imperial ambition, but the failure of an individual — even one as extraordinary as Guiscard — to bring about such a goal. If the content was *ungeheuer* as Kleist put it — extraordinary, but perhaps also a bit uncanny — what sort of a "form" or "shape" could it be given?

Tragedy or Trauerspiel?

In a letter written to a friend some two years after he had first heard Kleist read from his Guiscard fragment, the writer and critic Wieland recalls his initial response as follows

> I have to confess that I was amazed, and I don't believe that I am exaggerating when I assure you that if the spirits of Aeschylus, Sophocles and Shakespeare came together to write a tragedy, it would be what Kleist's *Death of Guiscard the Norman* could be, if it could correspond to what at the time he allowed me to hear (R 34–35).

Wieland had no doubt that Kleist's text was on the way to becoming the German equivalent of the greatest of tragedies. And there is little doubt that with the first and only completed act, Kleist had in mind the beginning of Sophocles's *Oedipus Tyrannos*. The point of departure that both works share is the affliction of their subjects by the plague and their call to their respective leaders to be saved from its ravages. But a comparison also brings out significant differences, which in turn reflect the difference between classical tragedy, on the one hand, and the modern *Trauerspiel* (literally: mourning play) on the other. Walter Benjamin makes a sharp distinction between tragedy and *Trauerspiel* in *The Origin of the German Mourning Play*, one that reflects the changed religious and cultural conditions out of which each emerged. Building on Franz Rosenzweig's analysis of tragedy as involving the refusal of the Self to submit to "mythical," that is, polytheistic, deities (here, Aeschylus' *Eumenides* is clearly the exemplary tragedy), Benjamin distinguishes classical tragedy from the modern *Trauerspiel*, which mourns the loss of a salvational promise by putting it into play. To examine this difference between tragedy and *Trauerspiel*, it is enough here simply to compare and contrast the situation in which both Oedipus and Guiscard find themselves with respect to the plague. But first their similarities. Both Oedipus and Guiscard are known for their prodigious intelligence: Oedipus, of course, for having solved the riddle of the sphinx, thus "saving" Thebes from destruction and being chosen as the city's ruler as a result. Guiscard establishes his rule through feat of arms, clever stragegy, and skillful political maneuvering. His name reflects not his ancestry — Hauteville — but rather, the cleverness he demonstrates. As one scholar writes, his "ingenuity, deviousness and lack of scruple soon gained him the nickname Guiscard ('the cunning' or 'the weasel')."[4]

We see already, however, that the two figures can be distinguished by the kind of intelligence ascribed to them. In the case of Oedipus, this involves what can be described as a generic intelligence, epitomized in the way he solves the riddle of the sphinx: by producing a single word that names an entire genre, "man." The intelligence ascribed to Guiscard, on the other hand, names a particular kind of cleverness, or "cunning;" it is intelligence as applied to singular situations, with which Guiscard as a warrior but also as a politician is constantly confronted. Military strategy calls not just for strength but for the understanding of unpredictable situations. This also distinguishes the behavior of Guiscard from that of Oedipus. Oedipus saves the city of Thebes and becomes its king. Guiscard establishes his fame through conquest and manipulation, and his rule in southern Italy must be maintained by military force. Guiscard is subjected, therefore, to a dynamic that recalls that of Athens as described by Pericles in his second discourse. He must extend his rule and try to establish an empire, or risk losing it. His campaign to conquer the Byzantine Empire by taking Constantinople can be seen in this light.

The reality of military expansion, however, belongs to the background of the actual texts, both that of Sophocles and that of Kleist. Both texts begin with groups of men coming to ask their leaders for help in escaping from the plague. But they do this in very different ways. First, the old priest who implores Oedipus:

> O ruler of my country, Oedipus! You see us lying down.... The town you see already totters, greatly, and can lift its head out of the pit no more and the red wave.... The plague ... empties Cadmus' house and hell grows rich with sighs and howling. *Now though I do not rate you like the gods ... still I do as the first in events of the world and in union with the spirits*[5] (italics added).

The priest does not consider Oedipus to be divine ("I do not rate you like the gods") but nevertheless considers him as "first" among equals "in events of the world." The Thebans come to the royal palace out of which Oedipus will then emerge to greet them.

What could be more different than the crowd of Normans who accompany Armin, their elder statesman, as it were, not to a palace, but to a tent, within which Robert will remain hidden for a good half of the act, as suspense builds about his condition? In Sophocles's tragedy, there seems never to be any question of Oedipus himself being subject to the plague. His malady is of a different nature and will be no less violent, if somewhat less destructive. In some versions of the myth, Oedipus kills himself at the end, but in Sophocles's theatricalization of it, he blinds himself in order to live on and find another end at Colonus.[6] In a very different way, the question of the end will also be the driving question in Kleist's play. But the topography of the scene as already noted is not that of a city and its citizens, but rather, an army camp engaged in a military campaign. The crowd of Normans, therefore, is not at home in a double sense. Although following a leader of Norman (and ultimately Viking) origin, they all are recent immigrants to southern Italy. This historical situation inflects the meaning of the final plea of Armin, with which the act either ends or breaks off: "Do not deny us Italy's celestial breezes / Lead us back, back, to our Fatherland!" (R 28). But what sort of a "fatherland" is southern Italy to these Normans? They are thus doubly estranged, first, from their Italian "fatherland," and second, from their Norman origins. For if one wishes to pursue their genealogy a bit further, we can recall that the name of their previous homeland, Normandy, derives from the fact that these groups came from the "north," as "North-men." The "Normans" were originally Vikings who settled "Normandy" in the eighth century and gave the region its name, before then two centuries later finding the area too small for their ambitions, which forced many to seek their fortunes elsewhere, some in southern Italy and others in England.

With this in mind, we can conclude that the history of the Normans, and especially the group to whom Robert Guiscard belonged, was one of conquest and migration, and what we encounter at the outset of Kleist's play represents both the high and low point of this history. The scene is a high point because it represents the closest the Normans, under Robert Guiscard, came to establishing their own empire. The low point ensues because this closeness would not be close enough, and indeed would lead to a disaster that recalls that of the Athenians in their ill-fated expedition seeking to conquer Syracuse, as recounted by Thucydides in Book 7 of his *History of the*

Peloponnesian War. This disaster is already palpable in the very first stage instruction of Kleist's play, which describes "the people" as "agitated movement" (*unruhige Bewegung*). They have come not just to demand that Guiscard call off his campaign and return home, but to use force if necessary to accomplish this end:

> It is with fervent prayers, you worthy fathers,
> That we escort you to Guiscard's tent.
> A cherub leads you, from the right hand of God
> When you go to shatter the rock
> against which the wave of an entire army,
> carried away with fear
> breaks and seethes in vain.
> Send a thunderbolt
> Upon that rock and open us a path
> To escape the terrors of this horror camp!
> Unless he quickly wrests us from the plague
> Sent us by hell, out of the sea this land
> Will rise as a burial mound for all his people (S 179, R 9).[7]

In both plays, we have a leader implored by his followers to save them from the plague, which is to say, from imminent death. But whereas in *Oedipus*, no one at first questions the power and legitimacy of the king, in *Guiscard*, revolt if not revolution drives the Normans' demands, and their aged speaker, Armin, must constantly strive to keep their agitation from exploding into open rebellion.

The underlying problem, which the plague both embodies and intensifies, is expressed again at the end in Armin's final plea to his leader:

> You know, o Lord—to whom is it more familiar?
> And upon whom does Destiny's hand lie as heavily?
> On your rapid flight, your breast aflame, toward the bed of the bride
> Your arms already reaching toward her and the nuptial rite
> Stepped, you bridegroom of the goddess of victory,
> The Plague gruesomely in between

To be sure, you say you are still untouched
But your people is empoisoned to the marrow of their loins,
Incapable of any more deeds
And daily, as pine trees before the storm wind,
Sink the heads of your loyal followers in the dust
The one who is laid low is without resurrection [*Der Hingestreckt' ist's auferstehungslos*],
And where he drops, he sinks into his grave (G 496–505, R 27).

In *The Origin of the German Mourning Play*, Benjamin describes the singular situation of the Baroque sovereign in a manner that also fits that of Robert Guiscard:

> As highly enthroned as [the sovereign] is over his subjects and his state, his status is circumscribed by the world of creation; he is the lord of creatures, but he remains a creature.[8]

The world of creation, to which Benjamin refers here, is in the Biblical perspective a fallen world of guilty, and therefore mortal, living beings. The plague, as Armin's discourse makes clear, imposes this realization upon even the most heroic of individuals and the most militant of peoples. For no war and no militancy can ignore the fact that "the one who is laid low is without resurrection" (*Der Hingestreckt' ist's auferstehungslos*). "Where he drops, he sinks into his grave." And, we must add, where he sinks, there he will stay. There is no resurrection. That is what the German baroque *Trauerspiel* mourns, and it is also why its form is radically different from that of Greek tragedy. The Greek tragic hero holds out the promise of a different, better world to come; for the hero of the *Trauerspiel*, this future is already past. And what makes it past, in Kleist's drama, is the sudden, abrupt, brutal intervention of the plague. Armin's final words could hardly be clearer in their very figurality. Robert is described as someone "flying" toward a victory that is designated through the trope of marriage nuptials: he is to be the "bridegroom" of the goddess of victory (*o du Bräutigam der Siegesgöttinn*). But the plague steps cruelly in between, blocking his way and "poisoning" his army. Military prowess, bravery, and cunning will not be enough to overcome this obstacle. He will remain forever a "duke," not a "king" or lord, because as a creature he is mortal, and as a mortal he can and will succumb to the plague. Oedipus, too, will die at Colonus, but with a promise of a better and different world. (We will return to that at the end of this study.) With Guiscard, that promise dies with him.

In other words, what makes *Robert Guiscard, Duke of the Normans*, precisely a *Trauerspiel* and not a tragedy, is that this death cannot, as with the tragic hero, be interpreted as a sacrifice that saves. "Der Hingestreckt' ist's auferstehungslos." For the one who is laid low, there is no resurrection. The unusual formulation in German calls attention to the institutional aspect of the situation. It is not that the fallen will not be resurrected, but rather that for the fallen — for mortals — there is no resurrection. It is the promise of resurrection itself that is no longer available. And it is precisely this — the demise of the promise of resurrection — that the *Trauerspiel* "mourns." Thinking back to Benjamin's *Origin of the German Mourning Play*, this statement expresses not just the despair of a character in the play, but rather the inability of the *Trauerspiel* to attain the goal of tragedy, as outlined by Benjamin, in which the sacrificial death of the isolated Self resonates with "distant new commands of the gods, and from this echo future generations learn their language" (110). This messianic, prophetic dimension constitutes the "frame" of classical tragedy and gives it its "power," which, Benjamin writes, is "one of the essential features that distinguish the ancient conception of life from the modern" (110).

In Kleist's fragment, that frame has lost the power that derived from its salvational promise. In the monotheistic, and above all, Christian culture that defined the modernity to which Benjamin refers, the Good News of a possible redemption and resurrection can be said to have become increasingly problematic, first with the split in Christianity — at the time of Guiscard, that between Constantinople and Rome — and then, at the time of Kleist, as a result of the Protestant Reformation. Guiscard's attempt to conquer Constantinople can be seen as an effort to overcome this split and thus to heal the fractured promise of Christianity as a Universal Church. His failure confirms that the division has become unbridgeable. The struggle with Islam, in which the historical Guiscard also took part, is only the external manifestation of the crisis of monotheistic universality, whereas the struggle between East and West churches, between Rome and Constantinople, is its internal manifestation.

If the salvational frame is thus irremediably fractured, the gap that it opens allows individuals such as Guiscard to make their way—up to a point. That point, however, is marked by the advent of the plague. As we have continuously stressed, the plague befalls not just individuals but also collectives. In so doing, it marks their interdependence but also the impossibility of a community that would surmount the limitations of finite, mortal individuals. The model that Christianity offers to overcome the gap between monotheistic universalism, with its promise of eternal life, and earthly individuals, is that of the Holy Family. If God can be conceived as producing a "son," who is thus able to redeem the guilt of mankind through his self-sacrifice, then the focus of Christian culture will have to be increasingly on the family as a possible redemptive "frame." The first and only act of Robert Guiscard demonstrates the necessity and also the impossibility of such a solution.

The Unholy Family

Perhaps it was in order to create a distance from this Holy Family that Kleist gave a certain importance to one of Guiscard's daughters, who received the name "Helena" precisely from the Greeks whom her father was seeking to conquer. In historical reality, she had been betrothed as a child to the young son of the then ruler of Constantinople, Michael, who, however, was shortly thereafter deposed and replaced by Alexius Comnenus. Helena was held hostage in Constantinople for a while until she was allowed to return to Italy. Kleist restores her to a position near her father on his final campaign. Of his two sons, historically named Bohemond and Roger, the former, as already mentioned, was forced to return to Italy in order to recover from an attack of the plague, whereas the latter had been sent ahead to Cephalonia in Greece, to prepare for the arrival of the armada. Helen is engaged to Guiscard's nephew, Abelard, who historically was constantly plotting against his father-in-law, although here he, too, has been integrated into the military expedition, where he plays a dubious role as the rival of Guiscard's son, Roger, here renamed Robert. Finally, Cecilia, the duchess and spouse of Robert, represents Guiscard's wife Gaeta, who historically only arrives on the scene in time to see her husband die of the plague.

The least that one can say about these family members is that they hardly present a heroic, much less a unified front when faced with the revolting Normans. Helena's first words, however, echo those of Oedipus in stressing the domestic, and indeed paternal, nature of the relationship of leader to followers: "You children of the best of fathers." But whereas Oedipus begins with similar words, "O you, old Cadmus' children, new offspring," the difference once again is immediately apparent. For Oedipus, the father is Cadmus, mythical founder of Thebes, a collective parent. For Helena, despite her Greek name, the "father" is her father, who, she reminds her people, has the right to sleep at night without being assailed by unruly soldiers. Oedipus assures the Thebans that he has come to listen to them firsthand; Helena rebukes the Normans for coming at all. However, in the face of their determination, she changes her tone and addresses them no longer as "children" but as "friends": "Won't you return later, friends?" (G 358). She finally agrees to the inevitable, letting them wait there in front of the tent until Guiscard appears: "Good, then, let it be, friends" (122).

The encounter with the son of Guiscard is hardly more encouraging. Kleist changes the name of Guiscard's first son from Roger to Robert, thus making him not just the direct heir of the duke but his namesake as well. This illustrates how a more secular Christian culture attempts to replace or supplement the uncertain promise of resurrection by translating it into domestic terms. If God the Father can live on in his Son, then perhaps humans can live on in their offspring

as well, particularly male. But the contrast, therefore, between the
warrior, Robert Senior, and his heir, Robert Junior, could hardly be
more drastic. Although the historical Roger fights with consider-
able success against the Byzantines, here Robert Junior tries simply to browbeat the old man who speaks for the group, and then to
intimidate the group itself in ordering them to leave. He particularly
shows himself disrespectful of the old man's—that is Armin's—age
and experience, thus putting his own ability to continue his father's
heritage all the more into question. Not only does he demand complete obedience from Armin, when he orders him to "take your troop
(*Schar*) away from this place" (S 184, R 17), he calls him a "gray fool"
and then allows himself to be provoked into a dispute by his rival,
Abelard, that further weakens and disgraces the family image before
its subjects. By betraying the dire situation in which Guiscard finds
himself, Abelard thus heightens the fears of the Normans and supports their desperate claim to call off the invasion and return to
their homeland.[9] That his interest here is ultimately personal and clan
power, rather than that of a larger collective, emerges when Abelard
challenges Robert's claim to be the legitimate heir to power:

> ABELARD: The ruler's son?—I am that as much as you.
> My father sat before yours on the throne!
> He did it with his fame, with more right:
> And more closely am I kin to the people (R 19, G 364).

Thus, while claiming the legitimacy of direct inheritance through his
father, Guiscard's brother, Abelard also cites "the people" as the ultimate source of his legitimacy. He claims to be "more closely . . . kin
to the people" than Robert Junior by supporting their demands to be
released and relieved from their military mission. In short, he allows
them to fear for their lives.

Retter in der Noth—Savior in Need

The act reaches its high point with the appearance of Guiscard, who
is greeted by Armin and the soldiers as a gift from heaven: "We salute

you, Prince, As though you came down to us from heaven, Since we thought you were already with the stars" (R 24). He appears as a kind of resurrection, and his affirmation that he is very much alive reassures his audience, if only briefly:

Your cheerful words

Returns a life to us we thought was lost

If only there were no grave that could cover you!

You would be immortal, Lord, immortal,

As Immortal as your deeds (R 24).

But despite his protestations, and his apparently triumphal appearance dressed in full armor, it is a silent gesture, indicated in a stage direction, that ushers in the final phase of the act:

Guiscard looks around, the old man stops speaking.

THE DUCHESS (*softly*): Do you want —

ROBERT: Would you like —

ABELARD: Is something wrong?

THE DUCHESS: God in Heaven!

ROBERT: What's wrong?

THE DUCHESS: Guiscard, say something!

The Empress grabs a large army drum and pushes it under him.

GUISCARD (*slowly sitting down, half-loud*): My dear child (R 27)!

This is the *Trauerspiel*'s equivalent of the stichomythia of tragic dialogue—the rapid exchange of short exclamations in a duel in which the participants joust with one another for supremacy. But here the short sentences are not self-contained. They are interrupted, anxious questions relating to something that is non-verbal: the bodily condition of Guiscard. In a gesture that could easily be staged as comic, the duchess pushes a "large army drum" under the sinking warrior, who "slowly" sits down on it.

This turning point demonstrates another of Benjamin's insights into the difference between tragedy and *Trauerspiel*: "The *Trauerspiel* is thinkable as pantomime, but the tragedy is not" (115). Another difference is the *Trauerspiel*'s proximity to comedy:

> The comic — more precisely the pure joke — is the indispensable inner lining of mourning, which like the lining of a garment at the hem or lapel, from time to time peeks out.... Seldom has speculative aesthetics been able to gauge how near the strict joke stands to what is dreadful (123-24).

Here, however, the "pure" or "strict joke" does not "stand" but sinks from a heroic stance into a mournful slouch, supported by an army drum that is otherwise used to accompany attacks and victories. The *Trauerspiel* is thus able to extract a moment of virtual mirth even from the horrors of the plague.

Signs of Guiscard's illness and approaching death break through the façade of strength he seeks to project, interrupting his discourse, making it impossible for him to continue standing, reducing his voice to a whisper. At this juncture, which comes immediately after Armin has announced that "the decisive moment" has come (R 27), the plague demonstrates a power that no army and no human effort can simply deny or ignore. For it is a power that reveals that its "pre-existing condition" of possibility is nothing other than the mortality of singular living beings, including humans of every rank and kind.

The militarization of human response to the plague displays its limits here. The very conditions that allow for maximal mobilization also permit the plague to take its course. The battle is an unequal one, as Defoe in his *Journal* recalls:

> It is not an ordinary strength that could support it, it was not like appearing in the Head of an Army, or charging a Body or Horse in the Field; but it was charging Death itself on his pale Horse.[10]

The horse of death is pale indeed, so pale that it hardly appears as such. What appears are its violent effects. And since the struggle is irreducibly asymmetrical, its violence seeks desperately for an object it can attack. In the absence of resurrection, this is how Armin at the end of the fragment describes its effects:

The one laid low is without a resurrection,

And where he fell, he sank into his grave.

He struggles, and again, with unsayable

Exertion to rise again; it is in vain!

And again he sinks into his grave.

Indeed in the horrific confusion of his senses

That befalls him in the end, one sees him

Bare his teeth against God and Man,

Against friend, brother, father, mother, children,

Raging against the bride herself, as she nears him (R 28).

Desperate rage, looking for an object, directed "against God and Man" and the rest of the family: this is the "stone" that the *Trauerspiel* of *Robert Guiscard, Duke of Normandy* leaves behind. The "savior in need"—*Retter in der Noth*, as Armin calls him at the end—can no longer respond to the desperate appeal, "Lead us back, back, to the Fatherland."

Or perhaps it is this very lack of a response that is a response—a response, but not an answer. But if so, it is the response of the *Trauerspiel*, not of a tragedy. It is a response historically focused on the individual. This focus will undergo a radical shift a century later when Antonin Artaud reflects on what in Kleist bordered on the comic: the relation of individuals to their setting; in other words on the relation of the theater to the plague.

CHAPTER EIGHT

Preexisting Conditions

(Artaud, "The Theater and the Plague")

"Acting Out an Agony"

Up to now we have been emphasizing that "the plague," despite its name, can only be studied in tandem with the "preexisting conditions" of the areas it affects as well as through the effects it produces. Although this aspect of the plague is largely implicit in most of the texts we have read, there is one in which it is not only explicit, but in which it tends almost to eclipse the plague as a self-present event. This eclipse enables Antonin Artaud to portray the plague as an immense, terrible, but also liberating experience—like that of theater. In what follows, we will try to explore the ambiguous implications of this little word "like" that returns so often in Artaud's text.

The essay, "The Theater and the Plague," was first presented in April of 1933 as a lecture held in the Sorbonne. Anaïs Nin, who was a friend of Artaud's, described the event in her *Diary* as follows:

> The light was crude. It made Artaud's eyes shrink into darkness, as they are deep-set. This brought into relief the intensity of his gestures. He looked tormented. His hair, rather long, fell at times over his forehead. He has the actor's nimbleness and quickness of gestures. His face is lean, as if ravaged by fevers. His eyes do not seem to see the people. They are the eyes of a visionary. His hands are long, long-fingered.
>
> . . . Artaud steps out on the platform and begins to talk about "The Theater and the Plague."

... It seems to me that all he is asking for is intensity, a more heightened form of feeling and living. Is he trying to remind us that it was during the Plague that so many marvelous works of art and theater came to be, because, whipped by the fear of death, man seeks immortality, or to escape, or to surpass himself. But then, imperceptibly almost, he let go of the thread we were following and began to act out dying by plague. No one quite knew when it began. To illustrate his conference, he was acting out an agony. ...

His face was contorted with anguish, one could see the perspiration dampening his hair. His eyes dilated, his muscles became cramped, his fingers struggled to retain their flexibility. He made one feel the parched and burning throat, the pains, the fever, the fire in the guts. He was in agony. He was screaming. He was delirious. He was enacting his own death, his own crucifixion.

At first people gasped. And then they began to laugh. Everyone was laughing! They hissed. Then, one by one, they began to leave, noisily, talking, protesting. They banged the door as they left. ... But Artaud went on, until the last gasp. And stayed on the floor. Then when the hall had emptied of all but his small group of friends, he walked straight up to me and kissed my hand. He asked me to go to the café with him.[1]

Much of Artaud's essay is condensed in this description. It is, above all, a performative work, not just because it was a lecture, but because it was about the plague as a certain kind of theater and about the theater as a certain kind of plague. But the particular relation of the plague to theater is not simple to describe. It is indeed at least double. Not just because later this text would be included in the volume of essays that would mark Artaud as one of the foremost thinkers of theater in the twentieth century, namely, *The Theater and Its Double*. The duplicity involved in linking the theater to the plague is condensed in Nin's description of his performance: "He was enacting his own death, his own crucifixion." I have previously suggested that it is not possible to "enact one's own death" in the strict (and important) sense, because death is the end of all enactment. What one can enact is one's *dying*, and it seems as though this is what Artaud was doing on the "platform" of the Sorbonne. He had changed that site from a place where knowledge was to be transmitted to a stage in which something very different was taking place—something that involved knowledge but that also exceeded it, in the traditional sense at least. Nin describes it precisely, when she notes, "He wanted to make people aware that they were dying," but also "to force them into a poetic state."[2] At the same time, as we have heard, she insists that "He was enacting his own death, his own crucifixion." If death cannot be enacted, a crucifixion certainly can. Indeed, it is perhaps the act *par excellence* because in being enacted, it is both itself and more than itself. The crucifixion represents not just a process of putting people—usually criminals—to death by affixing them to a cross, but also a sacrificial gesture. It then becomes a deliberate, voluntary dying that is intended to put death to death, at least virtually, and in so doing, to recover life. This is the intention that drives "The Theater and the Plague."

Anaïs Nin, who so perceptively describes Artaud's performance, also identifies its decisive turning point when she writes that at a certain moment, "imperceptibly almost, he let go of the thread we were following and began to act out dying by the plague." Artaud may have "let go of the thread we"—that is Anaïs Nin and the audience—"were following," but it is questionable to say, as she does, that he let go of the thread that *he* was spinning, since that thread was precisely "to act out dying (by) the plague." But it is a *theatrical* death that is being "acted out," and it fully conforms to what Anaïs Nin herself has just described as Artaud's intention, which was to communicate a certain "intensity," namely, that which results when "whipped by the fear of death, man seeks immortality, or to escape, or to surpass himself." Such a theatrical death is not simply fictional, in the sense of unreal, but rather frictional, in the sense of retaining elements of reality without being the same as what it represents. The three moments that Anaïs Nin mentions not only coexist with one another; they collide and conflict. They involve the search for "immortality," the desire to "escape," and the attempt to "surpass" oneself. What is being "escaped" is clearly a certain set of conventions and traditions; what is being "surpassed" is the "self" that those traditions support and stabilize. But what then about "immortality"? This responds directly to "the fear of death," but it responds to it by taking its major characteristic — its negation of temporal finitude — and inverting it, turning the eternity of nonexistence into a positive quality of the "self." For to speak of "immortality" is generally to imply the immortality of an individualized "self." The traditional way this contradiction is resolved, both in Christianity and in its secular heir in a certain aestheticism, is to distinguish between a physical or earthly self and a spiritual or heavenly soul. The physical self may perish, but the spiritual soul survives. This tendency will be very prominent in "The Theater and the Plague," where Artaud repeatedly strives to give what he calls a "spiritual physiognomy" of the plague, and indeed, to a certain extent to spiritualize it. However, where there is theater, the bodily element cannot be simply transcended. This produces a tension that runs through the entire text, and which its initial presentation in the Sorbonne apparently staged and embodied to the extreme. Its "embodiment" seems to have approached its disembodiment — a kind of negative incarnation that recalls and calls into question the notion of a "crucifixion" as the model for the overcoming of self. What, however, becomes of the singular living being when it is thus called upon to "overcome" itself by a theater that is "like" the plague but not simply identical with it?

One response becomes legible in the concluding words of Artaud's lecture, which ends with a question:

> And the question we must now ask is whether, in this slippery world which is committing suicide without noticing it, there can be found a nucleus of men capable of imposing this superior notion of the theater, men who will restore to all of us the natural and magic equivalent of the dogmas in which we no longer believe.[3]

Given the date of this lecture, April 6, 1933, it is hard not to think of the events that were taking place in Germany following Hitler's accession to power two months earlier. It is uncertain if Artaud had this particular "nucleus of men" in mind at the end of his lecture, even if some years later, in 1939, while interned in an asylum, Artaud will write a letter addressed to Adolf Hitler — never sent — expressing a certain solidarity with his cause.[4] But independently of his (phantasmatic) relation to the German Führer, the question remains whether Artaud's search to find a replacement for "the dogmas in which we no longer believe" does not easily — if not necessarily — lead in the direction of a charismatic leader directing a small "nucleus of men" in order to impose a "superior notion" of theater as a substitute or complement of religion. And if so, what would be the "role" played by the plague in this project? Is it the plague that makes possible this "superior notion" of theater; and if so, to what is it superior?

The Plague: A Political Dream

To begin to respond to these questions, it may be helpful to recall the discussion of the plague of Michel Foucault in *Discipline and Punish*. Against a certain tendency to see the plague as installing an almost carnivalesque situation in which "fear and death overcome prohibitions," Foucault emphasizes an almost opposite effect it provokes, namely, what he calls the "political dream of the plague," which is to say, a repressive, state-enforced "disciplinary mechanism":

> Against the plague, which is a mixture, discipline brings into play its power, which is one of analysis. A whole literary fiction of the festival grew up around the plague: suspended laws, lifted prohibitions, the frenzy of passing time, bodies mingling together without respect.... But there was also a political dream of the plague, which was exactly its reverse: not the collective festival, but strict divisions, not laws transgressed, but the penetration of regulation into even the smallest details of everyday life through the mediation of the complete hierarchy that assured the capillary functioning of power.... The plague as a form, at once real and imaginary, of disorder had as its medical and political correlative discipline.[5]

Although Artaud's notion of the relation between plague and theater is obviously closer to the "literary fiction" described by Foucault than to the "political dream" of establishing total discipline, it also seeks to elude the polarity that Foucault invokes. For Artaud, theater may imply a certain "festive" aspect, but it is neither simply joyous nor simply "fictional" in the sense of something that is exclusive of and opposed to "reality" or "politics." Artaud's theater is both fictional and political insofar as it entails implications for the *polis* and the polity.

This is why, when Foucault alludes to the plague as a "mixture," he seems closer both to Artaud and to what I have previously designated as "friction" rather than "fiction." Friction, unlike fiction, does not imply a simple alternative to existing reality but rather its more or less violent transformation. This transformation does not create a separate world of imagination, but rather coexists conflictually with the existing world it represents, transgresses, and exceeds.

If Foucault describes the disciplinary response to the plague as its "political dream," Artaud, too, begins with a dream, that of the viceroy of Sardinia, Saint Remy, in which he saw the plague "ravaging the whole of his tiny state" (15). But unlike the political dream described by Foucault, the dream of the viceroy conveys information not just visually or intellectually but corporeally. It is a dream that moves to action precisely by seizing the body: the body of the viceroy in order to predict its effects on the body of the city he governs. The body politic and the singular body of the viceroy are both submitted to a double movement in the dream; the collective body politic is submitted to an extreme disintegration. "Before such a scourge, all social forms disintegrate. Order collapses," writes Artaud. Morality is infringed, psyches unhinged. The singular body of the dreamer — the viceroy —*feels* that it is undergoing a similar disruption of its normal functioning: "Torn, failing in a dizzying collapse of tissue, his organs grow heavy and gradually turn to carbon" (15). What is solid dissolves, and what is liquid congeals. One thing, above all, for Artaud results from this tumultuous dream: the "will" which, he writes, "operates even in absurdity."

The dream itself is not a product of the will. It responds to a situation. But the will in turn responds to the dream, by leading the viceroy to make a momentous decision against the advice of all of his councilors, who are concerned more with economics than with survival. Responding to the dream, the viceroy decides to ban the ship bringing the plague from docking at Cagliari. His order is "considered irresponsible, absurd, idiotic and despotic by the public and by his own staff" (16). Nevertheless, he holds to it and orders the ship, the *Grand-Saint-Antoine*, to change course "and make full sail away from the town, under threat of being sunk by cannon shot. The Viceroy symbolically declares war upon the plague" (16). Through this decision, based on his reaction to his dream, he saves his island from the plague.[6]

The fact that Artaud chooses a dream to introduce his essay on "The Theater and the Plague" is not accidental. As much as he will emphasize the importance of the will in responding to the plague and to its effects, and as much as he will also insist on a certain notion of consciousness as part of that response, what is decisive is precisely that both will and consciousness are understood as intellectual faculties that *respond,* rather than simply attempt to dominate or to create. This is the significance of the dream: the dream brings to the viceroy a vision that he experiences not just mentally but physically, and to which he then responds decisively, even impulsively. He is ready to fly in the face of conventional wisdom, values, and priorities, which in this particular case, as subsequently in Marseille, involves the influence of powerful economic interests concerned with amortizing the goods being brought by the *Grand-Saint-Antoine* that were part of a thriving and profitable textile trade. In short, Artaud's introduction has nothing to do with a "literary fiction" that would be unrelated to "reality" or that would attempt to turn its values on their head, but rather with a vision that defends the health and safety of Sardinia by challenging the economic interests that would override those considerations and that indeed do precisely this when the ship arrives at Marseille, thus triggering the explosion of the plague not just in the city but subsequently in all of Provence.[7] Given the importance of the plague for Artaud's following argument, as a model for theater, it is significant that he begins by recounting the story of the viceroy who precisely saves his island from the plague.

However, to make things even more complicated, it is not simply the ship that brings the plague to Marseille. For as Artaud writes, the plague "was already there. And at a point of particular recrudescence. But its centers had been successfully localized" (16). In other words, the outbreak of the plague, was triggered by the arrival of the *Grand-Saint-Antoine* — the name of the vessel recalls Artaud's own first name — but it must be understood as interacting with preexisting conditions. And this, Artaud continues, "inspires certain thoughts" (16).

Before going on to list the thoughts thus inspired in Artaud, let me add one of my own, inspired by his text although not stated explicitly in it. If it is true, as it seems, that it was the collusion of economic and political interests in Marseille that was responsible for the vessel being allowed to dock and to unload its cargo without observing the otherwise stringent sanitary rules in force, then this would confirm an observation made by Anaïs Nin in her interpretation of Artaud's performance:

> For him the plague was no worse than death by mediocrity, death by commercialism, death by corruption which surrounded us. He wanted to make people aware that they were dying. To force them into a poetic state (192–93).

One of the preconditions for the outbreak of the plague in Marseille in 1722, despite its being previously contained and localized, would have been what Nin calls "death by commercialism." Again, this is not something that Artaud explicitly states, but his text implies as much.

The "thoughts" it "inspires" in Artaud may be listed as follows, not necessarily in the order that he brings them. "Between the Viceroy and the plague a palpable communication, however subtle, was established," and therefore, "it is too easy and explains nothing to limit the communication of such a disease to contagion by simple contact" (17). We have seen from his description of the viceroy's dream that this communication passed as much by the body as by the mind. Artaud notes that "the particular strength . . . this dream exerted upon him should be remarked" (16). The viceroy's decision could thus be called a "gut" decision in the most literal sense, since it derives not from a commercial calculation of profit and loss, but from a singular physical experience, one not determined by direct contact, and yet from which he draws consequences for himself and for the body politic. This thought alone distinguishes Artaud's approach to the plague from that of most of the other texts we have read, since he insists on a "palpable if subtle communication"—palpable because it passes by way of a bodily experience; subtle because direct contact is absent.

Artaud, who has read many of the canonical descriptions of the plague, is fully aware of how his position differs from them:

> If one wished to analyze closely all the facts of plague contagion that history or even memoirs provide us with, it would be difficult to isolate one actually verified instance of contagion by contact, and Boccaccio's example of swine that died from having sniffed the sheets in which plague victims had been wrapped scarcely suggests more than a kind of mysterious affinity between the flesh of the pig and the nature of the plague, which would call for more precise investigation (18–19).

Here two points can be made. On the one hand, Artaud's refusal to see "contagion" as a simple matter of physical "contact" seeks to open the possibility of other factors playing a role in the spread of the plague. Instead of "contact" and "contagion," he argues for a "communication" that is physical without being entirely material. This leads him to introduce the notion of "force." Commenting on the rapidity with which the plague decimates the 180,000-man Assyrian army in one night, thereby "saving Egypt," as recounted both in the Bible and in Herodotus, Artaud concludes that "we should have to consider the scourge as the direct instrument or materialization of an intelligent force" (18), one which destroys but also saves.

It is here that Artaud's relation to the religious tradition he also criticizes becomes apparent. Although fifteen years later he will author the unforgettable text and (initially censored) radio play, *Pour en finir avec le jugement de Dieu*[8] (*To Finish Up with the Judgment of God*), it seems clear that the author of "The Theater and the Plague" is already struggling with that judgment. To try to explain the spread of the plague as "the direct instrument or materialization of an intelligent force," even if he immediately adds that this force is presumably "in close relation to what we call fatality," does not diminish what Heidegger might call a certain "ontotheological" framework in which he is situated.[9] Artaud concludes: "I believe we can agree upon the idea of a malady that would be a kind of psychic entity and would not be carried by a virus" (18).

Of course, not everyone can agree that the plague or pandemics involve "a kind of psychic entity" that "would not be carried by a virus." But as we shall see, Artaud's conception of the plague is more complex than the notion of a "psychic entity" (much less an "intelligent" one), might suggest.

"*The Theater, Like the Plague . . .* "

If, as Artaud repeats again and again in this essay, "the theater is *like* the plague," this is not to say that the theater *is* the plague or that the plague *is* theater. It is rather to suggest that the two quite different phenomena share certain traits but also differ in others:

> If the theater is like the plague, it is not only because it affects important collectivities and upsets them in an identical way. In the theater as in the plague there is something both victorious and vengeful: we are aware that the spontaneous conflagration which the plague lights wherever it passes is nothing else than an immense liquidation (27).

Although the metaphor of the plague as a fire recurs in many texts on the plague, for instance, in Luther's constant reference to a house that is set alight,[10] the reference to a "spontaneous conflagration" seems to recall Boccaccio's remark comparing it to "a fire that will catch dry or oily materials when they are placed right beside it."[11] But whereas Boccaccio uses this image to demonstrate how the plague could be "spread by the slightest contact," Artaud emphasizes precisely the reverse: the "spontaneous conflagration" does not even need direct physical contact to ignite. There is a "communication" at work that must be understood differently, one that is mediated by what we have throughout been calling "preexisting conditions." Here is one of the most suggestive of Artaud's descriptions of those preexisting conditions, by virtue of which the plague "communicates":

> The plague takes images that are dormant, a latent disorder, and suddenly extends them into the most extreme gestures; the theater also takes gestures and pushes them as far as they will go; like the plague, it reforges the chain between what is and what is not, between the virtuality of the possible and what already exists in materialized nature. It recovers the notion of symbols and archetypes that act like blows of silence, organ points, stoppages of blood, summons of the lymph, inflammatory images thrust into our abruptly wakened heads. The theater restores to us our dormant conflicts and all their powers....
>
> In true theater a play disturbs the senses' repose, frees the repressed unconscious, incites a kind of virtual revolt (which moreover can have its full effect only if it remains virtual) (27–28).

After listing the many traits — above all, physical, visceral — that the plague and theater have in common, Artaud still insists that there is a decisive and significant difference between the two. In true theater, the "revolt" of the bodily senses and functions must remain "virtual" if it is to have its full effect. A murder shown on the stage should not incite the actor to commit it as an actual fact. The contrast here is between theatrical virtuality and the actuality of the plague. They are easy enough to confound in reading Artaud's text, because both play themselves out on the stage of the body. And both trigger a "revolt" that in a sense is already brewing, but dormant:

> But whereas the images of the plague, occurring in relation to a powerful state of physical disorganization, are like the last volleys of a spiritual force that is exhausting itself, the images of poetry in the theater are a spiritual force that begins its trajectory in the senses and does without reality altogether. Once

launched upon the fury of his task, an actor requires infinitely more power to keep from committing a crime than a murderer needs courage to complete his act, and it is here, in its very gratuitousness, that the action and effect of feeling in the theater appears infinitely more valid than that of a feeling fulfilled in life (25).

What Artaud here calls the "gratuitousness" of the acts performed on the stage is what distinguishes them from the consummated action performed in reality, whether that of the murderer or any other. Once they are fulfilled, as with the act of the murderer, such acts "exhaust themselves," whereas that of the "tragic actor remains enclosed within a pure and closed circle" (25). But this metaphor of the "pure and closed circle" is somewhat misleading, since it suggests a closure that is precisely also open: actual and virtual simultaneously.[12] By being closed off, the act is prevented from "exhausting" itself and its meaning in a single accomplishment or fulfillment. It thus retains a *signifying and affective potential* that, paradoxically, propels it beyond its own closure; or, as Artaud puts it, in a phrase that recalls certain arguments of Benjamin's in his *Critique of Violence*:[13]

> That murderer's fury has accomplished an act, discharges itself, and loses contact with the force that inspired it but can no longer sustain it. That of the actor has taken a form that negates itself to just the degree that frees itself and dissolves [it] into universality (25).

The theatrical "act" or "actor," although physically present on the stage, is never entirely "actualized," never fully present precisely because s/he is on the stage and coexists with it. The stage relativizes the actor, because he, she, or it signify something other than their immediate bodily existence. But the indirectness of this bodily existence remains one of the decisive traits that distinguishes theater from other artistic and medial modes and also links it to the plague without making the two simply identical.

The plague attacks both the body of the individual and the body of the existing society. But Artaud goes to great pains — without being entirely convincing — to argue that the ravages the plague wreaks on the body do not simply destroy it. Rather, he argues, they transform it in a distinctive manner. Artaud ends his gory description of the plague's effect on the body (which I will spare you here) by drawing two conclusions about its physical effects:

> The first is that the plague syndrome is complete without gangrene of the lungs and brain, the victim dying without the putrefaction of any member at all. Without underestimating the nature of the disease, we can say that the organism does not require the presence of a localized physical gangrene to determine its own death.
>
> The second observation is that the only two organs really affected and injured by the plague, the brain and the lungs, are both directly dependent upon consciousness and the will. We can keep ourselves from breathing or from thinking.... We cannot control the filtering of body fluids by the liver or the redistribution of blood by the heart and arteries.... Thus the plague seems to manifest its presence in and have a preference for the very organs of the body, the particular physical sites, that are closely related to human will, consciousness, and thought, which are in the process of manifesting themselves (21).

According to Artaud, "the plague seems to ... have a preference for the very organs of the body ... where human will, consciousness, and thought" are involved. The organs that it affects, the brain and the lungs, are most associated with conscious activity. But this conclusion follows a description of the attack of the illness in which it overwhelms the individual victim, completely eliminating any deliberate action of the will or any conscious thought:

> The victim scarcely hesitates to become alarmed before his head begins to boil and to grow overpoweringly heavy, and he collapses. Then he is seized by a terrible fatigue, the fatigue of a centralized magnetic suction, of his molecules divided and drawn toward their annihilation. His crazed body fluids seem to be flooding through his flesh. His gorge rises, the inside of his stomach seems as if it were trying to gush out between his teeth. His pulse ... at times slows down ... a mere virtuality of a pulse, at others, races after the boiling of the

fever within, consonant with the streaming aberration of his mind. . . . Every-thing proclaims an unprecedented organic upheaval (19).

Whatever else one can say about this description — and I have con-densed it, leaving out some of the more violent passages — it certainly does not suggest anything like the interaction between two intelli-gent forces. Rather, if there is a "mysterious affinity," as Artaud spec-ulates, it is between conflicting, asymmetrical forces. But however dissimilar those forces may be, their struggle is not entirely arbitrary. As we have noted in commenting on the Biblical plagues, Artaud retains an element that distinguishes the plague's dreadful power from that of other "natural" calamities, namely, the fact that it uses the mechanisms of the bodies it attacks to disrupt and destroy their normal functioning. "Body fluids" become "crazed," the circulation of blood is driven to extremes — "at times slows down . . . at others races" — bodily processes accelerate, producing a fever that reaches a boiling point, as the frantic rhythm of the heart becomes "conso-nant with the streaming aberration of [the] mind." Artaud compares this "unprecedented organic upheaval" with the "earth struck by lightning," except that with the plague, the violence comes not just from without but from within, "like lava kneaded by subterranean forces, search(ing) for an outlet" (19). And yet in this disruptive and ultimately destructive process, the struggle is not entirely one-sided:

In most cases a violent burning sensation, localized in one spot, indicates that the organism's life has lost nothing of its force and that a remission of the disease or even its cure is possible. Like silent rage, the most terrible plague is the one that does not reveal its symptoms [traits] (20).

This is entirely consistent with Defoe's observation of how physi-cians seek to bring the buboes or boils to burst, in which case there is a chance of saving the afflicted person. At the same time, in try-ing to pierce the hardened boils, they inflict enormous pain on the victims.[14]

But Artaud's descriptions, or rather fantasies of the plague, although by no means simply arbitrary, are not always consistent with the conclusions he draws. Thus, he describes how "in certain cases . . . the injured lungs and brain blacken and grow gangrenous. . . . The brain melts, shrinks, granulates to a sort of coal-black dust" (20). Immediately thereafter, however, he goes on to assert that the plague "syndrome is complete without gangrene of the lungs and the brain," as already quoted. On the one hand, he asserts that "there is neither loss nor destruction of matter, as in leprosy or syphilis" (20). On the other, he describes such destruction in brutal detail. It seems as if he is tempted to portray the plague not just as an enormously destructive force, but also as one that undertakes its destruction possibly in order to purify: "The buboes appears wherever the organism discharges either its internal rottenness or, according to the case, its life" (20).

The problem, we see here, is that such purification (and the word will return frequently toward the end of the essay, in relation to the theater) seems inextricable from the destruction of what it is purifying. The "organic upheaval" is so complete that it leaves little left to survive the process of "purification." Indeed, from a material point of view, the process looks more like one of pulverization. To repeat a passage already quoted: "The softened and pitted lungs fall into chips of some unknown black substance — the brain melts, shrinks, granulates to a sort of coal-black dust." The process may also resemble one of calcification: "The gall bladder . . . is full, swollen to bursting with a black, viscous fluid so dense as to suggest a new form of matter altogether. The blood in the arteries and the veins is also black and viscous.[15] The flesh is hard as stone" (20).

What pulverization and calcification, two of the extremes involved in the "organic upheaval" produced by the plague, have in common is their resistance to individuation. In other words, what the plague disrupts and destroys, is the capacity of individual living organisms to maintain themselves. The "immense liquidation" referred to earlier has as its aim the dissolution of individualized organisms, and in the process, the liberation of vital forces that can no longer be restricted or constrained within individual entities.

Artaud similarly describes its effects on collective life, as organized in cities. These places are the sites of collective, social life, and even if they are not simply society itself, they provide the conditions under which society operates. The plague disrupts and destroys these conditions; unfortunately, the English translation misses the decisive term here: "Once the plague is established in a city, *les cadres réguliers* — the regulative frameworks (and not, as in the published version, "the regular forms") — collapse" (23). The French word, *cadre*, has a number of different meanings, including most literally, "frame," but also denoting upper administrators as well as the environment, surroundings, setting: that which defines and delimits a place or an institution. For this reason, I would prefer to translate it as "framework," since it also includes "the frames of reference" through which thought and action is organized. Indeed, as with the bodies of individuals, here, the body politic and the body of society become unhinged. Note how Artaud in the following account describes the "collapse" of the "frameworks":

> There is no maintenance of roads and sewers, no army, no police, no municipal administration.[16] . . . Then wood, space, and flame itself growing rare, there are family feuds around the [funeral] pyres, soon followed by a general flight, for the corpses are too numerous. The dead already clog the streets in ragged pyramids gnawed at by animals around the edges. The stench rises in the air like a flame. Entire streets are blocked by piles of the dead. Then the houses open and the delirious victims, their minds crowded with hideous visions, spread howling through the streets. The disease that ferments in their viscera and circulates throughout their entire organism discharges itself in tremendous cerebral explosions (23).

Individual living bodies become heaps of corpses, blocking the circulation of the survivors — a kind of social embolism. The "disease that ferments" within the bodies produces "tremendous cerebral explosions." The oppositions that keep society and individuals stable, separating mind and body, private and public, life and death, break down together with the "regulative" and "regular frameworks" that ordinarily sustain such oppositions and allow people and institutions to situate themselves with respect to them.

In this situation of extreme collapse of traditional frameworks, there occurs an event that provides Artaud with the link between the plague and the theater:

> The dregs of the population, apparently immunized by their frenzied greed, enter the open houses and pillage riches they know will serve no purpose or profit. And at the moment theater takes over (24; translation modified).

Once again, I have had to change the published translation, which reads "And at that moment, theater is born." Theater is most certainly not "born" at that moment, since, like the plague, it already is there. But what happens is that it takes over a scene that is already becoming a violent and disorganized spectacle. Artaud writes, dramatically: "*Et c'est alors que le théâtre s'installe*," literally, "It is then that theater *s'installe*." *S'installer* can mean "to move in" or to "install oneself," to set oneself up. But since this is also a highly conflictual moment, I prefer "takes over." In any case, what defines this decisive moment where the theater suddenly appears is that it is a moment in which private property becomes an object not of self-definition or aggrandizement but of pure passion: the poor who pillage the houses of the rich do so not in order to profit from the wealth of the privileged, but for the pure pleasure of violating the rules that separate private from public property. They do it — like Augustine stealing a pear, as he describes in Book II of his *Confessions* — knowing full well that it "will serve no purpose or profit." For the theater that so installs itself — takes over — is one that is based on the "immediacy of gratuitousness provoking acts without use or profit." Such acts, therefore, retain their signifying potential because they are not "exhausted" in the actualization or accomplishment of a goal or purpose. They remain open.

And these acts give a very different significance to the notion of Artaud's account of the plague as an "intelligent force" that we

cited earlier. Intelligence now is precisely not goal oriented, not organized around the aggrandizement of the organism or the organization, whether individual or collective. Rather its essential incompletion recalls Defoe's melancholy musing about how the imminence
of death causes people to forget their private passions and come
together without imposing their sense of self and their values upon
others. Artaud's "communication" in this sense can also be related
to Boccaccio's emphasis on "compassion" as the framework of the
Decameron. Or finally, it even resonates with Luther insisting on the
obligation one has to help one's "neighbor." And yet Artaud goes perhaps one step further than his predecessors, since he refuses to interpret this suspension of self-oriented values provoked by the plague as
being the simple result of the fear "of immanent death," and therefore of the "absence of sanctions" that such imminence brings with
it. This, he argues, does not "suffice to motivate acts so gratuitously
absurd on the part of men who did not believe death could end anything." Nor can this "explain the surge of erotic fever among the
recovered victims who [try] to wrench a criminal pleasure from the
dying or even the dead" (24). For the plague has not created anything
radically new, but only revealed and reactivated (17) something that,
like the "virus" in Marseille, was already there, a preexisting condition. To describe this condition, Artaud once again invokes the relation of the plague to theater:

> The state of the victim who dies without material destruction . . . *is identical
> with* the state of an actor who is entirely penetrated by his feelings that also
> overwhelm him without any profit for reality [*que ses sentiments sondent inté
> gralement et bouleversent sans profit pour la réalité*] (24; italics added).

This is one of the rare, if not the only, place in this essay where Artaud
abandons his comparison of theater and plague, signaled by the word
"like" (*comme*) or the reference to "analogy," and instead collapses the
difference into identity. It should be superfluous to counter that the
"state" of someone who is dying of plague is not "identical" with that
of an "actor," no matter how much the two may have in common.

Elsewhere in his text, Artaud is careful to preserve this distinction, but here he allows it to recede before the affinity of the two "states." Without accepting this statement at face value, one can and should note that it is indicative of the importance of the particular affinity involved, namely, the state of being saturated or transfused (*sondent*) by feelings that "overwhelm him without any profit for reality." The plague cuts off its victims from that which normally determines their relation to reality — above all, self-interest — by condemning them to death in the same way the theater cuts off the actor from reality by suspending any relation of feelings or passions to self-interest. But, of course, the actor generally survives, whereas the victim of the plague generally does not.

In his passion to bring out the profound affinity of the plague to theater, what Artaud thus occasionally overlooks, is the decisive difference between the two. Both overturn the "frameworks" that order and organize a particular social reality and the lives of individuals living in it. But whereas this overturning of the theater retains a decisive "virtuality" with respect to the "actuality" of ordinary "reality," the ravages of the plague eliminate the indispensable condition of both virtuality and actuality themselves, namely, the existence of singular living beings. It is because Artaud, like many others, cannot or will not distinguish between a social order and an organic order that he refuses to acknowledge fully the difference between the virtuality of the theater and the lethal actuality of the plague.

Ultimately, what allows him to collapse this distinction is a notion of "spirit" that he inherits from the Christian tradition he so adamantly opposes but still perpetuates.[17] It is not by accident that the major authority that he invokes in this essay is Saint Augustine, and precisely the text from *The City of God*, which Artaud quotes at length, where Augustine condemns theater and lauds Scipio for having outlawed it:

> "Know," he says, "you who are ignorant, that these plays, sinful spectacles, were not established in Rome by the vices of man but by the order of your gods. It would be more reasonable to render divine honors unto Scipio than to such gods. . . .

If there still remains among you sufficient trace of intelligence to prefer the soul to the body, choose what deserves your reverence; for the strategy of the evil Spirits, foreseeing that the contagion would end with the body, seized joyfully upon this occasion to introduce a much more dangerous scourge among you, one that attacks not bodies but customs" (26).

For Artaud, it is Augustine's condemnation that demonstrates insight into the true nature of theater. The plague attacks only the body, of individuals and of collectives, whereas theater attacks their "customs," which is to say, the traditions and values that transcend the limitations of finite individual lives.

Individuals, for Artaud here, are understood as the subjective correlative of organized society, and as such, based on repression, exclusion, and constraint. And yet, as he suggests in his discussion of John Ford's *Tis Pity She's a Whore*, individuals are indispensable also to his notion of theater. For it is the individual, Annabella and her lover, Giovanni, who sacrifice their lives and their bodies to give what Artaud calls "an example of absolute freedom in revolt," providing an exemplary "image of absolute danger" (29).

The word "absolute," that Artaud repeats here, should be taken as literally as possible. For what emerges from this exemplary example of the theater as plague is the readiness of individuals to sacrifice themselves, which is to say, to destroy what is constrained and limited in them by the social and by the organic order. They sacrifice this to what Artaud calls their "passion"—the word again echoing, not accidentally, the passion of Christ. But where Christ allows himself to be executed by others, Giovanni performs the executions all by himself: first of Annabella, whose body he dismembers, then of his rival, and finally of himself. In this orgy of blood-letting, in which killing converges with self-sacrifice and self-affirmation, Ford's play, as Artaud writes, "resembles the plague's freedom" through which:

the agonizing victim [*l'agonisant*] inflates [*gonfle*] his character [*son personage*], where the living [*le vivant*] gradually becomes a grandiose and overextended being [*un être grandiose et surtendu*] (30).

Artaud's use of a rather unusual French word, *surtendu*, to sum up the "grandiose" figure that Ford's play stages, is almost untranslatable. "Overextended" does not fully communicate the extreme and indeed excessive "tension" that the word designates, literally, a kind of "hypertension." The underlying excess here — the *sur* that drives the "tension" to the breaking point — results from Artaud's effort to conceive of the "inflation" or swelling (*gonflement*) of the "character" in the play — which recalls the swelling the plague produces on the bodies of its victims — as being something more than the self-destruction of the individual subject. This image of "absolute danger," thus, by virtue of its very absoluteness, cannot be detached from the impossible image of a monotheistic god, from whose "judgment" Artaud seeks to extract society through theater — and the plague.

The "spiritual physiognomy" that he seeks to construct of theater as plague thus remains tied to this notion of the Absolute, even when it is negativized in the form of an absolutely self-destructive "passion." This "spirit," however, also remains tied to the body it consumes. This link between spirit and body, between the spiritual and the Absolute, complicates the conclusion Artaud seeks to give to his essay. At its end, Artaud proclaims his hope that theater, like the plague, will be understood and practiced not just as "a poison" but as "a redeeming epidemic" (31). He wants to believe that "the theater like the plague is a crisis which is resolved by death or cure," which is to say, by "death or an extreme purification." But the purification is so extreme that it converges with death itself. It liberates from "the hypocrisy of our world" and "the asphyxiating inertia of matter" (31) only by providing the breath of death in the cries and gestures of the dying.

And as in the Christian tradition, to which Artaud is as indebted as is Nietzsche, there is an ultimate culprit:

> The theater, like the plague, is in the image of this carnage and this essential separation. It releases conflicts, disengages powers, liberates possibilities, and if these possibilities and these powers are dark, it is the fault not of the plague or the theater, but of life (31).

The ultimate culprit is "life" itself, which is guilty of "this essential separation." But this guilt can relate only to the life that is inscribed in "all the magnificent Fables which recount to the multitudes the first sexual division and the first carnage of essences that appeared in creation" (31). This fable recounts a life that would or should exist before and after all separation, and yet paradoxically acknowledges its "guilt" in order to proclaim its original innocence.

The plague, then, like Artaud's theater, takes its revenge upon this life of guilty innocence by confronting the living with what those fables have encouraged "the multitudes" to forget: a "separation" that is prior to all guilt because it is an "essential" precondition of the living. This is the "counter-fable" that Artaud leaves us to decipher. One such attempt at deciphering this guilty innocence is at the origin of what is perhaps the most famous novelistic recounting of this experience, which the author had initially thought of calling "The Separated," but to which he finally gave the title, *The Plague*.

CHAPTER NINE

Confinement

(Camus, *The Plague*)

> Rieux had nothing to look forward to but a long sequence of such scenes,
> renewed again and again. Yes, plague, like abstraction, was monotonous.
> –Camus[1]

What is involved when a writer takes an event as destructive as "the
plague" and "fictionalizes" it, that is, inscribes it in an account that
both makes specific reference to really existing places and times and
at the same time recounts something that clearly did not occur? It is
precisely this situation that provokes the passage from Daniel Defoe
that Camus chooses as the epigraph for his novel, although it is not
retained in the English translation: "It is no less reasonable to represent one kind of imprisonment by another than it is to represent
anything that exists really by something that does not."[2] To represent
something existent by something nonexistent is "reasonable" when
the two share properties that transcend simple factual existence.
That property, if we are to follow Defoe, is "imprisonment." And
since the imprisonment that will be represented in the novel is a
result of "the plague," it is the relation between the two that justifies the fictional substitution. Just what is being substituted by the
fictional plague has been an object of controversy. The most obvious
candidate has long been recognized as the Nazi occupation of France,
which occurred at the time Camus was writing the novel (starting in

1941–42). The fictional plague would thus legitimately represent the historical fact of the occupation of France and Europe from 1941 to 1944, insofar as both could be seen as instances of a certain "imprisonment." Seven years after the book's publication in 1947, Roland Barthes challenged this approach as a *malentendu*, a misunderstanding, with the following argument:

> No structure in *The Plague*, no cause, no connection between *The Plague* and an elsewhere that could be the past and other places, in a word, no construction of relations [*point de mis en rapport*].[3]

Interpretation of plagues has rarely produced anything like unanimity. Writing in 1955, eight years after the book's publication in 1947, Roland Barthes argued that this equation was a misunderstanding, since in the novel, the plague, deprived of any sort of history, becomes merely a foil against which a "moral of friendship" can emerge, whose subjects are marked more by "solitude" than by "solidarity." Camus responded to Barthes in an open letter, in which he defended the historical content of his novel:

> *The Plague*, which I wanted to be readable from several angles [*qu'elle se lise sur plusieurs portées*], has as its evident content the European resistance against Nazism. . . . *The Plague*, in one sense, is more than a chronicle of the resistance. But it is certainly that as well [*Mais assurément, elle n'est pas moins*].[4]

Here is not the place to enter into the long debate that pitted Barthes (as well as Sartre and much of the French Left) against Camus regarding this novel, and more generally, Camus's political and ethical position. It is sufficient, I think, to recognize that whatever might have been Camus's initial inspiration in writing the novel, looking back upon it, he emphasizes that he also "wanted [it] to be readable from several angles" (*sur plusieurs portées*), even if he considered its "evident content" to be "the European resistance against Nazism." In his letter, however, Camus reasserts the legitimacy of using "the plague" to represent not just the Nazi Occupation of France but all "tyranny":

> No doubt I am reproached for allowing *The Plague* to serve all the resistances
> to all tyrannies. But . . . I cannot be accused of refusing history except if one
> declares that the only way of entering into it is to legitimate tyranny (547).

In short, what qualifies *The Plague* as "historical" is the struggle
between the events it narrates and the resistance to "tyranny." The
plague, in short, becomes a figure of tyranny, and this is what allows
the struggle of the persons who "resist" it to represent those who
resist historical tyrannies, whether that of Nazi occupation, or that
of Soviet imperialism, which was surely also on Camus's mind in
the post-War period. The question, then, that Barthes's critique and
Camus's response raises concerns the legitimacy of fictionalizing
"the plague" as a representative of a political event, namely "tyranny."

Camus has a relatively simple and straightforward response to
this challenge: "The proof is that this enemy, which was not named,
was recognized by everyone and in all the countries of Europe" (546).
To be sure, the novel insists on the use of police to reinforce the
confinement with which the authorities seek to contain the plague.
But beyond the fact that the Occupation and, in general, wars share
with plagues a certain lethal violence, Camus does not elaborate on
the differences we have been remarking on throughout our discussion of previous texts. Like wars, plagues affect collectivities, not just
individuals, and also provoke some sort of collective response. But
unlike war, plagues are not the result of intentional acts, or at least
not initially and primarily. Even if the acts that lead to and prevail in
wars turn out to be misguided and to produce very different results
from what they had intended, they remain dictated by deliberate,
more or less calculated strategies. Moreover, the response to the
plague of Rieux, as a physician, is also that of someone simply doing
his job, exercising the profession he has chosen. He may be doing it
selflessly, courageously, even "absurdly," given his limited ability to
influence the course of the disease, but his spirit and that of those
who are helping him is hardly that of one who is "resisting" a foreign
invader or tyrannical rule. To equate the plague with "tyranny" is to

endow it with the same kind of will and consciousness that informs political rule, tyranny or not. But is the plague conscious, and does it have a will? To think of it that way is what Dr. Rieux will early on describe as the "humanist" error — and his "fellow citizens" in Oran were, according to him, precisely such "humanists":

> In this respect our townsfolk [*nos concitoyens*] were like everyone else [*tout le monde*], wrapped up in themselves [*ils pensaient à eux-mêmes*]. In other words, they were humanists: they did not believe in calamities [*fléaux*]. A calamity is not made to the measure of man (37/41-42).

I will return to this passage later on. Here at the outset, however, we can raise the question of whether or not the metaphorization of the plague as an equivalent of both "tyranny" in general, and of the Nazi occupation of France in particular, does not perform the same anthropomorphizing that Rieux attributes to "humanists"? And that this thereby deprives the "calamity" of its distinctive, non-human character? It also, perhaps, deprives it of its all too human aspect as well, if, as we have been discussing, plagues never take place in a vacuum but are always co-determined by "preexisting conditions" — conditions that are not necessarily universal or generalizable from one plague event to another, even if the responses to the plague retain certain characteristics over the ages.

Like most comparisons, Camus's suggested equation of "plague" with "tyranny" is more interesting for the differences it reveals than for the similarities. One of the things that might have suggested the comparison could have been the phrase used in French in the 1930s to describe the rising tide of Nazism: the "brown plague" (*la peste brune*), where the color refers to that of the shirts of the SA. But what about the plague itself? As a highly infectious and deadly disease, it could represent the rapidity with which Nazism was able to "infect" masses of people, first in Germany, but later in other parts of Europe as well (particularly following its initial military successes in the West). One of the major preexisting conditions of its success was, of course, the economic disaster brought about by the Great Depression, and the apparent success of Nazi Germany in providing full employment for its citizens. Like the plague, the "brown plague" depended upon preexisting conditions for its success. But this similarity also reveals irreconcilable differences. For the masses it infected, Nazism (and also Fascism more generally) was able to generate and put on displays of mass enthusiasm and often intense loyalty. By contrast, in Camus's Oran, the arrival of the plague hardly produces the kind of enthusiasm that the annexation of Austria did. No one welcomes the plague once they are compelled to admit that it has arrived. The only similar mass demonstration occurs at the end, when the plague has receded, and it will give the narrator, Dr. Rieux, an opportunity to distance himself from the crowds and leave his readers with a final "lesson" (*enseignement*). Here is how he describes that "lesson":

> For he knew what this joyous crowd ignored, and that one could read in books, that the bacillus of the plague never died or disappeared, that it could remain dormant for dozens of years in furniture and linens, that it waits patiently in bedrooms, cellars, suitcases, handkerchiefs and papers, and that, perhaps, the day would come when for the misfortune and instruction [*enseignement*] of men the plague would awaken its rats and send them to die in a happy city [*une cité heureuse*] (308/278).

The novel ends with the profession of this "knowledge": Rieux "knew" what the crowd ignores, namely, that the plague might subside, but it would never simply disappear for all time.

This time- and history-transcending power of the plague is what it shares with the Defoe epigraph to the novel. As quoted or translated into French, Defoe speaks not of "prisons" but of "imprisonment." The difference is not insignificant. Prison is a thing; imprisonment is a process. It is ongoing and therefore cannot be construed in terms of a determinate present. In short, it goes on, virtually, even where it is not obvious, manifest, or to use Camus's own words, "evident." The plague is anything but "evident." What then about the novel of this title?

If Camus insists that the "evident content" of the novel establishes its relation to Nazi occupation, which is to say, to a determinate historical event, while at the same time rooting that event in more general, perhaps universal, human conditions, then it can be argued that this "evident content" may well operate in the manner that Freud attributed to the dream. In his *Interpretation of Dreams*, Freud distinguished between what he called the "manifest" content of the dream and its "latent" content, arguing that the former not only does not exhaust the dream's significance but, in fact, does everything to conceal it. This Freudian distinction does not merely repeat the traditional opposition between appearance and reality, since both contents can be said to have their own "reality." The reality of the manifest content is that it functions to conceal conflicts that must remain hidden, inaccessible to waking consciousness (i.e., self-consciousness), if the dream is to be remembered without having a traumatic effect. Despite the famous formula of "the dream is a wish-fulfillment," the wish "fulfilled" by the dream cannot be displayed directly. For the dream is driven by conflicts, not just by wishes, and these are often so violent that were they to be revealed as such, they might well challenge the unity of the ego, of its sense of itself, in an extremely disruptive way. This is why the latent content must be concealed, or rather revealed but only in an indirect manner. Could the same possibly hold for Camus's text, *The Plague*? That is, could its generalizing metaphorization of "the plague" not be a way of distracting from something else that is more powerfully at work driving not the dream, but the novel?

Replacing one sort of imprisonment with another, and even one sort of existence with another one that is nonexistent, as suggested by the epigraph from Defoe, requires there to be a *tertium comparationis* that allows the exchange to take place — which means *in the same place*, as it were. Something takes the place of something else by occupying its place, which remains unchanged. The plague that did not take place in Oran in the 1940s — was a fiction, and historically non-existent — replaces the plague that did take place in France at the same time, which, although existent, was not really a plague at all, despite the label of the "brown plague." Indeed, that label distinguishes what took place in France from what happens in the novel in Oran for two reasons. First, the "brown plague" may have involved the use of extremely violent and lethal force to impose itself, but the fact remains that it did not impose itself entirely through those means. It gained adherence through widespread consent and through its ability to improve the lives of many of its citizens. It was no doubt a "tyranny," but it also had the adherence of many of its subjects. If it was a "prison," it was not felt to be that way by huge masses of peoples that saw it as the only viable alternative both to capitalism and to communism. Even in occupied France, in the early 1940s, there was widespread support for the collaborationist regime of Marshall Pétain. Thus, neither the notion of "imprisonment" nor that of the "plague" can provide the common denominator allowing the justification of the "replacement" of an existing prison by another, fictional one.

Rather, there must be something about the site that enables the replacement to occur and that explains the relation between imprisonment, plague, and tyranny. It is, therefore, entirely consistent that the novel should begin with a description of that place:

> The curious events that constitute the subject of this chronicle took place in 194., in Oran. It was generally thought that they were out of place there, where they seemed somewhat extraordinary. At first sight Oran is, indeed, an ordinary city and nothing more than a French prefecture on the Algerian coast (3/11).

The events referred to — soon to be identified as the plague — are described as "curious," not just because the place and approximate dating permit one to know that no such events actually did take place in the city named during the decade indicated.[5] The events are "curious" because "it was generally thought that they were out of place." But generally thought by whom? To whom does this general impression refer? Surely, the statement refers to the inhabitants of that "happy city" who will joyously celebrate the end of the plague at the end of the novel and who will be masters of self-deception, according to the disabused narrator, Dr. Rieux. But Oran is described in a very general way as lacking specific distinctions or merits, as being entirely "ordinary" so that only its administrative status can be used to identify it, as "nothing more than a French prefecture on the Algerian coast." As nothing more, but also as nothing less. Perhaps for Camus, writing in Nazi occupied France, the fact that a French prefecture was situated "on the Algerian coast" could seem entirely "ordinary." The French, after all, considered themselves to be victims of a colossal aggression, of the "brown plague" that imprisoned them in their own country. That they, on the other hand, could possibly be in a different posture in Algeria, establishing a prefecture on its coast, is something that apparently did not disturb or disrupt the banal normalcy of Oran. It was no doubt "generally thought" that it was entirely normal for France to exist on both sides of the Mediterranean, at least in the 1940s.[6] But "generally thought" by whom?

The question is not explicitly raised in the novel beyond attributing such "general thinking" to those the narrator repeatedly refers to as *mes concitoyens* ("my fellow citizens") and not, as the English translation by Stuart Gilbert would have it, "the townsfolk." But if "my fellow citizens" could be considered as synonymous with "the townsfolk," this could relate to a distinctive feature of the city of Oran. The population of Algeria at the time, about ten million, was 90% "indigenous" to use the term employed by the French colonial administration, that is, mostly Arab and Berber, whereas only 10% were of European extraction. But in Oran, by contrast, the population was about evenly divided between Europeans and non-Europeans. This set it apart from the rest of Algeria. While the Europeans resided mainly in the central parts of the city, the non-Europeans lived on the outskirts or in a circumscribed area known to the Europeans as the *village nègre* (the "negro village") although actually very few Africans lived there.[7] This name suggests that no distinction was made between the Arab-Berber population and the population of Africa as a whole. In the words of the French colonial administration, they were "indigenous," and, above all, non-European.

In his memoir on "Oran and the Plague," Denis Guénoun, who
was born in Oran and who lived there until adolescence, recalls how
clearly defined and separated the non-European population was from
those of European descent, and, of course, not just in terms of residence. He even goes on to suggest that the motif of *separation* names
one of the essential aspects of the plague in the novel. He does not
mention that Camus had at first planned to call his novel *Les séparés*
("The Separated") and only later decided on *The Plague*.[8] This is usually taken as referring to the biographical situation of Camus during
that period. He had left Oran in 1942 and gone to France to be treated
for tuberculosis and then was stranded there by the allied invasion of
North Africa in November of that year. Camus was not to return to
North Africa until the end of the war.

But the motif of separation is not simply biographical. Rather, as
Guénoun convincingly argues, there was another more collective
separation that is barely visible in the novel but that is nevertheless
legible in the text, namely, the separation of the European (mainly
French) community from the non-European population in Oran.

But if "separation" usually suggests a spatial distancing, then it can
be argued that the motif of separation, which is emphasized throughout the novel, functions in a way that recalls Freud's description of
the manifest content of the dream, namely, to distort and conceal
conflicts. For the separation between the two communities in Oran
and in Algeria involved not just spatial distancing but economic and
political subjugation. The latent significance of the motif of separation, then, would be *exclusion:* exclusion of the non-European community from political, economic, and cultural equality. This situation antedated the plague, but it was solidified and stabilized by it.
Describing the situation of the city in the immediate aftermath of
the plague, the narrator seems to want to hold its advent responsible
for the sense of exile felt by its inhabitants:

> At the end of the plague, with its misery and privations, these men and women
> had come to wear the aspect of the part they had been playing for so long,
> the part of emigrants whose faces first, and now their clothes, told of long

banishment from a distant homeland. Once the plague had shut the gates of the town, they had settled down to a life of separation (298/145).

But who after all are "these men and women" who "had come" to assume "the part they had been playing for so long," and who felt themselves as "emigrants" and exiles "from a distant homeland"? The plague is described as having brought confinement and separation, but were they not already there? For the plague as described in the novel merely continues a separation that had emerged ever since the French militarily conquered Algeria in the mid-nineteenth century, namely, the separation of the European from the non-European community, but also the subordination of the latter. The suffering described in the novel, as a result of the plague, obscures the exclusion that defines colonial rule in general but also the very particular situation of Algeria and of Oran, namely, the exclusion of the major part of the population from equal civil, political, cultural, and economic rights.[9]

This exclusion of the non-European community, however, is by no means airtight. On several occasions, the novel alludes to the conditions of such exclusion as part of the colonial mentality and situation. I will mention two here. The first occurs when "an odd scene that took place at the tobacconist's" is recounted:

> An animated conversation was in progress and the woman behind the counter started airing her views about a murder case that had created some stir in Algiers. A young commercial employee had killed an Algerian on a beach.
>
> "I always say," the woman began, "if they clapped all that scum in jail, decent folks could breathe more freely" (54/27).

The allusion is first of all to Camus's earlier, first novel, *The Stranger*, which recounts precisely such a murder, although here the event is reflected through the attitude of the tobacconist, "a woman by the way," as it is specified shortly before the anecdote is related. Although the words of the female tobacconist are not without ambiguity, it seems more than likely that the "scum" (*racaille*) she denounces refers not to the European murderer, but to his Algerian victim. This is one of the very few occasions when non-Europeans are mentioned at all in the novel. A second time occurs later in the novel, when a naval officer recounts a story about a typhus epidemic he experienced in Cairo:

> "They had camps, you know," he was saying, "for the natives, with tents for the sick ones and a ring of sentries all round. If a member of the family came along and tried to smuggle in one of those damn-fool native remedies, they fired at sight. A bit tough, I grant you, but it was the only thing to do. (154/76)

The only non-European victims of the plague mentioned are those outside not just of Oran but of Algeria — in Cairo, where they are placed in "camps," under military guards who "fire on sight" if the confinement is violated. "A bit tough, I grant you, but the only thing to do," according to the naval officer, just as the tobacconist seems to blame the Algerian, who is murdered, rather than the European who kills him. And since the former incident is also a self-reference to the author's earlier work, it may be read as an indication of his awareness of the violence that marks the unequal relation of force between colonizers and colonized.

However, these two incidents are presented on the margins of the main plot, as segregated from it as are the two communities from one another. By confining the plague to Oran — a so-called ordinary French city on the Algerian coast — the narrative of the novel reproduces not just the perspective of the plague as imprisonment, but also of colonialism as not just separation but exclusion and subordination. In comparison with earlier accounts of the plague, Camus thereby eliminates one of its most distinctive traits, which is precisely its power to defy such confinement even while producing it. This is also the characteristic of colonialism and of empires as well.

Moreover, it is not just "the plague" that imprisons, but the response of the ruling authorities to it. This is yet another problem with equating or conflating the plague with "tyranny," since it tends to efface the specific conditions under which institutions function

politically. Once again, in the novel, the effects of institutional violence are mentioned, but never developed. The political dimension
of the confinement and its violence require police and military force.
Periodically, sounds of gunfire are described, but without being further localized. This gives them an indeterminate generality that converges with the tendency to abstract from concrete conditions and to
universalize. In any case, Camus's narrator does not display the same
curiosity as does Defoe's. And this is consistent since in the end he
claims to know what is going on. He does not need to see for himself.

What he and we as readers are given to "see" is carefully fictionalized to meet the demands of the "secondary elaboration." In this
case, secondary elaboration involves making the city as such, independently of its social relations, the cause of the confinement. Denis
Guénoun, who as mentioned grew up in Oran, is able to reveal how
this works:

> The whole plot is founded on the fact that the city is isolated in a sort of state
> of siege.... A severe military vigilance is instituted at its gates, in order to
> prohibit all passage. Except that if I am not dreaming, the town of Oran at
> this time did not have any kind of "gate" where one could control those enter-
> ing and leaving. And for a simple reason: such gates are only conceivable for
> a fortified city.... But in the post-war years there were no fortifications, no
> walls capable of isolating the city.

This remark, indicating the direction in which Camus "fictionalizes" the city of Oran to become a place of confinement, can be
contrasted with Thucydides's description of the Athenian project of
constructing a protective wall, which became one of the major *casi
belli* in provoking war with the Spartans. But no such construction is
described in the novel. The walls and gates are simply presented as a
given reality to suit the demands of the fiction.

Here, however, we have an excellent example of how a "fiction"
becomes what I prefer to call a "friction": the separation, exclusion, and ultimately fortification are on the one hand presented in
the novel as a "given" characteristic of the city and on the other as

quasi-direct actions of the plague, whereby the political institutions are neutralized as relatively direct effects of the pandemic. If the institutions are violent, the "separation" they enforce is presented as resulting from something that itself is "separated" from all mediating "preconditions." All, that is, except the equally isolated individual Europeans who constitute its cast of characters. As a result, what Guénoun, but also Rieux, calls "separation" is presented as a purely intra-communal distancing of individuals rather than as the imposition of exclusions that institute and perpetuate domination.

Perhaps the most flagrant sign of this exclusion of exclusion can be found in the reiterated use in French of the word "*concitoyens*" by the narrator. As already mentioned, the process of naturalization that is already at work in the French text is intensified by the Gilbert rendering of the word as "townsfolk." The problem is that the French word refers specifically to the status that was denied to the non-European half of the population in Oran, and to 90% of the Algerian population as a whole, namely, full citizenship. This denial, of course, has its history. Algeria was integrated into France in 1848 as a *département*, but from the start, the non-European population was excluded from the rights that normally came with such integration. This political violence continued the violence that decimated the Algerian population during the period of the French conquest. It is estimated that "between 500,000 and 1,000,000 Algerians out of a total population of 3,000,000 were killed by the French due to war, massacres, disease and famine." And in the very period that Camus was writing his novel, in March and April of 1945, the French massacred some 30,000 Algerian Arabs who were celebrating the end of the war and demonstrating for greater autonomy.[10]

All of this highlights Guénoun's conclusion:

> In the story the closing of the city functions in a manner strictly equivalent to the absence of Arabs. The Arabs are the exterior of this imaginary city, in the exclusion of which it has enclosed itself. The image of the fortifications in which the city is enclosed (and of the gates it requires) is purely fictive.

To that I would only add that this image of fortifications is not only "purely fictive," but also "frictional," insofar as it involves not just the *replacement* of something existent by something nonexistent, but their conflictual and significant *coexistence*: the coexistence of the real, historical city of Oran, which lacked fortifications, with the nonexistent city whose fortifications allow it to contain and concentrate the plague and its effects. Thus, what Camus via his Defoe epigraph refers to as the replacement of an existing imprisonment by one that is nonexistent but fictionally significant, functions not as a simple substitution but as one that involves conflictual coexistence. Such coexistence is frictional insofar as it de-universalizes and de-allegorizes its references precisely by remarking the significance of their non-convergence. Such non-convergence prevents its components from having a univocal meaning. In this way, as friction, the novel calls attention to the conflicts preventing the emergence of a unified meaning. In respect to Oran, this invests the closure of its "gates" or *mes concitoyens* with a significance that both transcends and negates their denotated meaning. What is not mentioned explicitly — the inexistence of gates in the real city, or the exclusivity of the *con-* in *mes concitoyens* — renders the terms significant beyond their immediate meaning. This excess marks the omission of exclusion without developing its ramifications to the point where they would call into question the status of the narration.

But there is a third occasion where reference is made to the condition of the Arab population, and it is significant because it also establishes a link to the problematics of the plague. Early on in the novel the newly arrived journalist, Raymond Rambert, meets the narrator, Dr. Bernard Rieux, and explains to him why he has come to Oran:

> He was preparing a report for a major Parisian daily on the living conditions of the Arabs, and was interested in information concerning their sanitary situation. Rieux responded that their situation was not good. But before going any further, he wanted to know if the journalist could tell the truth.
>
> Certainly, said the other.
>
> I mean: can you publish a total condemnation?

Total, no, I have to admit. But I suppose that such a condemnation would be groundless (12/18–19).

Rieux does not reply directly to this self-justificatory remark of the journalist, but he refuses to share information with him as someone who is willing to make "concessions" to "injustice" (12/18–19). Rambert will never complete or publish his story, at least not in the novel, and he thus offers yet another instance where the power of the colonial state — this time over the press — is remarked but also left undeveloped. It may be invisible, but it is not illegible. This mixture of invisibility with legibility links its fate to that of the plague. For the plague, too, is invisible. It can be seen only in its effects and even then, not at first. For dead rats, and then dying human beings, need not in and of themselves be signs of the plague. It is only when they achieve a certain density, a certain intensity, when they increase so much that they both invite and defy accurate enumeration, that "the plague" begins to be suspected:

> Things went so far that the agency, Ransdoc [acronym for *renseignements, documentation* (Information-Documentation)] announced in its free-information radio program that six thousand two hundred thirty-one rats had been collected and burned in one day of [April] 25th. This number, which gave a clear meaning to the daily spectacle that the city had before its eyes, added to the distress (E16, F22).

Enumeration, we see once again, can appear to give "a clear meaning" to a spectacle of dying rats that announces the arrival of the plague. But when those numbers get out of hand, that "clear meaning" tends to cloud up, especially where what is being counted are no longer dead rats but dead human beings. As the reality of the plague begins to impose itself, Dr. Rieux struggles to, as we might say today, "wrap his head around it," which is to say, around numbers that tend to lose their meaning:

> But even when Dr. Rieux had to recognize before his friend that a handful of dispersed patients had just, without warning, died of the plague, the danger

remained unreal for him.... In looking out of his window at his city that had not changed, it was just barely if the Doctor felt stirring in him that light disgust before the future that one calls anxiousness. He tried to collect in his mind what he knew about the disease. Numbers floated in his memory and he said to himself that the thirty great plagues that history had known had made about 100 million dead. But what are 100 hundred million dead? When one has been in war, one hardly knows what a single death is. And since a dead person only counts if one has seen him dead, one hundred million corpses strewn throughout history are only haze for the imagination (37–38/42).

The plague remains unreal, haze for the imagination, since only what one can see and imagine is the measure of reality. The plague remains unreal for Dr. Rieux and even more for his "fellow citizens," since they cannot see it as such—not yet at least.[11] The repetitive sights and sounds of that life that one calls "everyday" reinforces this invisibility, whether of the plague, or of the situation of those whose exploited work and suffering make possible the relative comfort and prosperity of his "fellow citizens." The non-European community that remains largely invisible in the novel, and to his "fellow citizens," converges with another aspect of their lives that they equally refuse to recognize, their mortality:

What is more exceptional in our town is the difficulty one may experience there in dying.... Think what it must be like for a dying man, trapped behind hundreds of walls... while the whole population, sitting in cafés or hanging on the telephone, is discussing... discounts.... These somewhat random indications give perhaps a sufficient idea of our city (5/13).

It is to this particular exclusion—that of mortality through self-interested commercialism—that the plague puts a (temporary) end. Its disruption of the peaceful routine of the city thus allows it to be compared with war (one of the topoi in recounting the plague). But here as elsewhere, the comparison is illuminating in its divergences: "When one has been in war, one hardly knows what a single death is," Dr. Rieux muses. With the plague, by contrast, death is experienced as a threat both to the collective and to the individual. There is another factor that also undermines the comparison. In war, human beings kill one another more or less voluntarily. Death may come suddenly, arbitrarily, but it generally involves the intention to kill. The same cannot be said of the plague. This is what makes it so difficult to grasp using a frame of reference organized around so-called normal, that is, intentional, activities:

> In this respect our townsfolk [*nos concitoyens*] were like everyone else [*tout le monde*], wrapped up in themselves [*ils pensaient à eux-mêmes*]. In other words, they were humanists: they did not believe in calamities [*fléaux*]. A calamity is not made to the measure of man. One tells oneself therefore that the calamity is unreal, it's a bad dream that will pass. But it refuses to pass, and from bad dream to bad dream, what passes are humans, and first of all humanists, because they have not taken any precautions. Our fellow citizens were not more guilty than others, they forgot to be modest, that's all, and thought that everything was still possible for them, which supposed that the calamity was impossible. They continued to do business, they prepared trips, and they had opinions. How would they have thought about the plague, which suppresses the future, displacements, and discussions. They thought themselves free and no one will ever be free as long as there will be plagues (37/41–42).

It is illuminating to compare the attitude of *nos concitoyens*, as described here, with that of the Athenians as recounted by Pericles in Thucydides. Pericles celebrates the ability of the Athenians to meet all future eventualities through the liberty of their intellect and the audacity it permits. "The fellow citizens" of Oran are described quite differently, even if the narrator insists that they are, after all, like *tout le monde*, like everyone else. If so, this would suggest that the whole world is entirely "wrapt up in itself," in its plans and projects, its business enterprises, and its voyages. In French, this disposition is perhaps more striking: "they thought only of themselves" (*ils pensaient à eux-mêmes*). The obligation to one's "neighbor," on which Luther in his Letter insists, plays no great role here. "They thought themselves free," and in the process, "they forgot to be modest." The Greek word for that forgetfulness was, of course, hubris. But in the modern period, another word takes its place: guilt. "Our fellow citizens were not more guilty than others," Rieux muses, but perhaps also not less either. In the religious and cultural tradition to which Rieux and his fellow citizens largely adhere, "guilt" is linked to "death," but also to the hope of overcoming it, of putting death to death, in the words of Saint Paul or, in the words of Christ, to "Let[ting] the dead bury the dead" (Matt. 8:22). The living have other more important tasks to accomplish, especially if they hope to outlive their mortality and to overcome guilt through their liberty. But this sense of being free crumbles when it presupposes a mode of a living being that would be free of death itself. It is this that the plague challenges: it "suppresses the future" as a domain of infinite self-realization. And because of that, those who cannot or will not relinquish this idea of a self that can outlive its mortality refuse to prepare for that which will make their efforts futile. According to Dr. Rieux, these are the "humanists," who are most vulnerable to this return of the repressed because they have "taken no preparations."

Rieux's mention of "humanists" here seems a bit out of place. Yet, it still fits well with the tendency to self-absorption he attributes to his "fellow citizens," who think only of themselves and their projects and not of what they cannot see or will not acknowledge. In this viewpoint, a "humanist" is understood as someone who believes s/he can abstract from the singular experience of individuals in order to arrive at a conception of the experience of all: a generic experience. "My fellow citizens" think of themselves as living a normal and essentially human life, a category that they seek to fill with their projects, their "opinions," and their values. For them, the "neighbor" is the one who lives and thinks and speaks as they do; all others are either bad neighbors ("scum") or fools, who are and should be excluded, for instance, from "citizenship" and, above all, from view. And if they insist on no longer being so ignored, they will be treated as the enemy, to be destroyed or subdued, as the French did to the Algerians in the massacres of April and May 1945. In the famous scene from *The Stranger*, the main character, Meersault, meets an Arab on the beach, the brother of a woman with whom his friend, Raymond, has a relationship. The Arab, who has previously wounded Raymond, draws a knife, which dazzles Meersault with the reflected rays of the sun. Meersault, blinded by sweat and sun, draws a revolver and shoots the Arab dead. What is perceived as a lethal threat, followed by a moment of blindness, results in a killing.

The plague also kills, but without enmity. The relationship of the murdered Arab and Meersault is determined by a very specific history. The relation of the plague to its victims is as well, but its general precondition is human mortality. The plague confronts humans with the danger of imminent death, but this danger is experienced in very different ways, depending on how their society and culture relates to mortality. The way that Rieux's society relates to mortality emerges in a conversation he has with an "older colleague," Dr. Castel, who in the face of the mounting number of deaths admonishes Rieux:

> "Naturally," he tells him, "you know what it is, Rieux."
>
> "I'm waiting for the results of the analyses."
>
> "I know what it is and I have no need of analyses. I spent part of my career in China and I've seen several cases in Paris, twenty years ago. Only at the time one didn't dare give them a name. Public opinion is sacred: no panic, above all no panic. And then, as a colleague said, 'It's impossible, everyone knows that it has disappeared from the West.' Yes, everyone knew, except the dead. Come on, Rieux, you know as well as I do what it is."
>
> Rieux reflected. Through the window of his office he saw the side of a stony cliff that in the distance closed upon the bay. The sky, although blue, had a dull sheen that became ever softer as the afternoon progressed.
>
> "Yes, Castel," he says, "it's almost incredible. But it does seem to be the plague."
>
> Castel got up and went toward the door.
>
> "You know how they will react," says the old doctor. "It has disappeared from countries in the temperate zones for years."

"Disappeared? What does that really mean?" responded Rieux, shrugging his shoulders (35–36/39–40).

Just as the Oranais refuse to see the other half of their "fellow citizens," they also refuse to acknowledge or even name the danger that is approaching. They prefer to think that it has disappeared "from the West." The question that Rieux poses to Castel at the end of their conversation applies not only to the plague: "Disappeared? What does that really mean?" The poor, the homeless, the impoverished—all tend to "disappear." This helps many of "our fellow citizens" to think of themselves as comfortably safe and secure. But it is no accident that Dr. Castel knows otherwise. For he has worked in China and is not bound by the self-absorbed and defensive opinions that determine attitudes in Oran. In the topography of the novel, it is significant that Rieux from his office can look out of his window at the bay, where a stony cliff "closes" its half-circle on a distant horizon. For in terms of visibility, it is the ocean that most powerfully challenges the self-absorbed normalcy of Oran:

> On the other side of windowpane, the sound of an invisible tramway suddenly echoed and refuted in a second the cruelty and the suffering. Only the sea, at the end of a dingy checkerboard of houses, bore witness to everything troubling and never at rest in the world (40/44).

It is this sea, and that to which it bears witness — everything troubling and never at rest in the world — that the "normal" city of Oran has turned its back on, once again in the hopes of creating a safe and self-enclosed haven:

> This city, unpicturesque, without vegetation and without soul ends up by seeming restful. . . . It is only fair to add that Oran is grafted on to a unique landscape, in the center of a bare plateau, ringed with luminous hills and above a perfectly shaped bay, with the result that it is impossible to see the sea, you always have to go look for it (6/13).

As with the sea, the reader has "to go look for" much of what is barely visible in the novel. Oran — or at least the *concitoyens* who run and dominate it — has turned its back on the sea, just as they have turned their backs on the non-European population and just as they try to turn their backs on the plague. It will not be seen until it is already too late to stop. "Oran" shields its view from the sea, as from death itself.

The plague brings death back into view. But it does not make visible that part of the hidden population that would suffer most from the disease, were it ever really to occur.

Denis Guénoun, in the article already cited, asserts, rightly, that "it would be childish to imagine that the absence of Arabs results from an *acte manqué*" on the part of Camus: an oversight or perhaps in a Freudian sense, a "slip" that conceals a conflict. We have already seen that the novel remarks on this absence on numerous occasions and implicitly suggests that what is at work is not merely an oversight but an exclusion. For Guénoun, "the absence of Arabs is not an error at the margins of the work" but rather "constitutes the subject of the novel." He links this to the motif of "separation," which I have tried to enlarge to encompass the notion of exclusion. From a Freudian point of view, this separation could be seen as a defensive act of "isolation." Isolation according to Freud is one of the "defense mechanisms" of the ego, which tries to defend its integrity by disassociating elements from their conflictual consequences. Freud adds that this process is difficult to separate from the more normal processes of "concentration," so necessary to everyday thought and action. Such isolation must be distinguished from repression, since it allows its object access to consciousness, but without allowing its consequences and ramifications to become visible. But like repression, and as with all "defense mechanisms," isolation leaves traces and has its own consequences. In the final section of this chapter, I want to argue that with respect to the novel, the most important of these consequences can be seen in the instability of the narrative perspective from which the story — and the plague — are recounted. Therefore, this perspective—ultimately a colonial perspective—constitutes both "the subject" and also "object" of the novel and thus is the "preexisting condition" of *The Plague*. The instability, however, reflects the unresolved and largely unacknowledged conflict between generality and singularity. The plague and mortality may be universal to all living beings; the "tyranny" of colonial exclusion is not. It is the unelaborated articulation of these two factors that both drives and unsettles Camus's narrative.

The unresolved tension of these two factors can be felt most keenly in a certain oscillation of the narrative and of the fictional-frictional narrator. In our previous discussions of texts recounting the plague, we have remarked how the plague demands both a third- and a first-person perspective, corresponding to the way it affects both individuals and the collectives in which they participate. From a temporal point of view, the third-person perspective corresponds to a position of the survivor, placing the events recounted safely in the past. Throughout the novel, the narrator describes himself as producing a "chronicle" and thus assumes a certain distance from the diversity of what he is recounting. But toward the end of text, he reveals himself to be identical with its main character, Dr. Rieux. Through this rather clumsy gesture, Camus seeks to establish a continuum linking a more or less omniscient third person narrator to the more partial and fragmentary first-person perspective. Stylistically, this gap is frequently bridged through the use of what in French is called *style indirect libre*, indirect free discourse. This is a form of narration in which the third-person position is maintained, while the content of the discourse expresses feelings and thoughts that indicate a first-person perspective. The ease with which the narrative moves from direct discourse to indirect discourse to "free indirect style" suggests a continuum between the plague as experienced by the narrator, the narrated, and the collective to which they all belong. But it is precisely the status and significance of this collective that is in question—that of *mes* (or *nos*) *concitoyens*—since as we have seen, the *con-* here excludes one half of the residents of Oran as well as nine-tenths of the residents of Algeria. And yet, despite this exclusion, the narrator can arrive at conclusions that imply a universality that ignores the partiality of the narrative. The narrator and main character can thus claim at the end of the novel to provide a conclusion that is also an *enseignement*, a lesson, to a "city" that is both blissfully unaware of the danger and moreover is "happy" in its ignorance.

But if it is a city to which the narrator belongs, it is also one whose limitations he does not fully acknowledge. Or rather, he acknowledges them as universally "human," but not as singularly "colonial." On the contrary, in "concentrating" his focus on this one city, in fortifying it by giving it walls that in reality it never had, he already "isolates" the plague and thus deprives it of one of its most essential characteristics, namely, its mobility. Plagues travel, and their infectious force is rarely limited to a single city. This, of course, is what governments try to accomplish with more or less success and historically often by means of confinement. But the question here is to what extent the narration does not make itself complicit with the very imprisonment that it seeks to invest with universal significance, announced through the epigraph from Defoe. The narration seeks to impose imprisonment not just as a specific, historically conditioned *preexisting condition*, but instead as a more or less universal characteristic of human life.

But is this project any different from what, according to the narrator, "humanists" do when they anthropomorphize the plague and thereby ignore the fact that there are calamities (*fléaux*) that are "not at the measure of man"? By blinding themselves to the specific, distinctive, and always singular conditions under which plagues function, such "humanists" are constitutively unable to deal with them as anything other than as the absolute limit of their "freedom": "They thought themselves free and *no one will ever be free as long as there will be plagues*" (37/41–42; italics added).

"No one will ever be free as long as there will be plagues;" but since there will always be plagues, it is perhaps better to avoid the either-or alternative of freedom or plague: life or death. For, as Rieux's old asthmatic patient observes at the end of the novel: "What does that mean — 'plague'? Just life, no more than that." No more, but also no less. That, however, this more or less cannot be detached from the always singular and non-universal traditions that endow human life with its irreducible singularity — this perspective informs the last author we will look at, Friedrich Hölderlin, in his highly idiosyncratic reading of Sophocles's *Oedipus* and the plague to which the king seeks in vain to respond.

CHAPTER TEN

Living with Plagues (Hölderlin, "Remarks on Sophocles's Oedipus")

A Lack of Modesty

Early in Camus's novel, *The Plague*, the main character and narrator, Dr. Bernard Rieux, describes the state of unpreparedness in which his "fellow citizens" of Oran found themselves at the outbreak of the plague:

> Our townsfolk were like everyone else, wrapped up in themselves. In other words, they were humanists; they did not believe in calamities (*fléaux*). A calamity is not made to the measure of man. One tells oneself that the calamity is unreal, it's a bad dream that will pass. But it refuses to pass, and from bad dream to bad dream, what passes are humans, and first of all humanists, because they have not taken any precautions. Our fellow citizens were not more guilty than others, they forgot to be modest, that's all, and thought that everything was still possible for them (*The Plague*, 37).

This is just one of the many rather sententious passages that fill this novel. But despite its moralizing tone,[1] it remains memorable, perhaps because of the unusual connection it makes between what Rieux calls "humanists" and calamities (*fléaux*: scourges). Extreme disasters, he suggests, are not easy to measure in terms usually associated with human life.[2] For if man is the measure of all thing — the humanist credo — such calamities fall outside what is imaginable. For Rieux, there is nothing unusual about this. We all judge things by relating them to what is familiar: "Our fellow citizens were no more guilty than others, they simply forgot to be modest." Such lack of "modesty," however, leaves those it afflicts particularly unprepared to deal with what exceeds the normal and familiar.

We have seen this at work in the responses to the initial outbreak of Covid-19, where many of those in a position of official responsibility, whether national or international, tended to explain their lack of preparedness by insisting that "no one could have predicted" the worldwide spread of Covid-19, whereas, in fact, such pandemics had in recent years been predicted with increasing insistency and not just by epidemiologists. The list of such predictions is far too long to list here. A book published in 2015 in France was entitled *The Return of Epidemics*,[3] and in the past few decades, there have been many such books, articles, movies, and video series stimulated in part by the emergence of AIDS, Ebola, SARS, MERS, Zika, Dengue, and many other highly contagious diseases. But the allocation of resources to improve national and international public health facilities to study and prepare for future pandemics was rarely a high priority for individual nations, except in certain areas that had previously been hard hit by one of these epidemics.

One such exception is Taiwan. Following the outbreak of SARS in China in 2002, Taiwan suffered the highest per capita mortality rate in the world from this disease. But as a result, the Taiwanese government created a Central Epidemic Command Center (CECC) to coordinate both governmental and civil responses, first to SARS, and then, seventeen years later, to Covid-19. Its success in dealing with the pandemic has been unique: as of November 27, 2020 the country, with a population of 23.5 million, had suffered only 7 fatalities due to the disease. Of course, Taiwan is an island and can thus control its borders perhaps more easily than most other countries. But its response to the outbreak of Covid-19 in Wuhan, in December of 2019, was effective because it was coordinated and because it enjoyed wide support among the population.[4] Mindful of Dr. Rieux's remark about the "lack of modesty" of his fellow citizens in a fictionalized Oran of the 1940s, the following remark in a recent paper reflecting upon lessons learned from Taiwan's Covid response is instructive: "Reflections upon past uncivil acts among citizens motivated the civil sphere to foster a discourse of interdependence, redefining the boundaries between individual choices and civic virtues."[5] Of course, as the authors acknowledge, a mere "discourse" is not enough if the social reality does not in some ways support the value of "interdependence" as a social and economic reality, and not just as a proclaimed "civic virtue."

"Gute bürgerliche Ordnung" *(Good Civil Order)*

What could it mean if the plague were to elicit a response in which "modesty" were not entirely forgotten? In such a case, Boccaccio's call for "compassion" and Luther's insistence on one's obligation to "the neighbor" would prevail over the panicked retreat into self-interest. In search of a possible alternative, we return to a play that we have already touched on in our discussion of Kleist's unfinished drama, *Robert Guiscard*, namely, Sophocles *Oedipus Tyrannos*. In our previous discussion we stressed the significant differences between the two openings: in *Oedipus Tyrannos*, the crowd of Thebans beg their king, who has saved their city once, to save it again, this time not from the sphinx but from the plague. Oedipus, who like Guiscard is known for his intelligence, tells them he has sent Creon to get advice from the oracle at Delphi. For the Thebans begging for aid, there is no question of confusing their king with a god: "I do not rate you like the gods," but only "as the first in worldly events," the Theban priest tells Oedipus, thus drawing a line that will prove to be decisive. The contrast with the attitude of the Normans at the beginning of Kleist's play could hardly be more striking. They approach their leader, Robert Guiscard, as the god that failed — failed to protect them from the plague that is decimating them. They come to their commander not just to entreat him to allow them to abandon his campaign and to return home, but with the threat of turning the violence they embody against their own leader if he refuses.

Thus, both dramas begin with a desperate cry to be saved from the plague. But the response that cry evokes could not be more different. In Kleist's play, the response is denial, first by the various family members of the commander, and then by Robert Guiscard himself. His denial that he has been afflicted by the plague, implying that he is probably immune to it, is undercut almost immediately by his near-collapse on the stage. Oedipus, by contrast, temporizes, hoping that Creon will bring him words of advice from the oracle. Oedipus's collapse is deferred to the end, and its gradual but irresistible approach constitutes the substance of the tragedy. Guiscard's collapse can only be held off until the end of Act I, which thus makes the rest of the play difficult to envisage not just for us but for the author. Kleist could not complete it. It remains the fragment of a *Trauerspiel*, demonstrating the human weakness of the sovereign, but not a tragedy, in which the ruler struggles with his fate before finally succumbing to it.

The tragedy of Oedipus, then, depends on how the words of the oracle are interpreted by Oedipus, to be sure, but when dealing with translations, also by the translator. The way the words of the oracle have traditionally been rendered, and therefore interpreted, can be exemplified by the following passage from the translation of E. P. Watling — a translation I have somewhat modified based on notes by the eminent classicist, Richard Jebb:

> CREON: There is an unclean thing (*miasma*)
>
> Born and nursed on our soil, polluting our soil,
>
> Which must be driven away, not cherished what is past cure.
>
> OEDIPUS: What unclean thing? And what purification is required?
>
> CREON: The banishment of a man, or the payment of blood for blood. For the shedding of blood is the cause of our city's peril.
>
> OEDIPUS: What blood does he mean? Did he say who it was that died?
>
> CREON: We had a king, sir, before you came to lead us. His name was Laius (1. 2:97–99).

This rendition of the oracle's words is roughly similar to that of almost all translators of the play, with one significant exception, to which I will come in a moment. In the conventional version, the message conveyed by the oracle is that the plague is an "unclean thing" — only one of the meanings of the Greek word used by Sophocles, *miasma*[6] — that has been "born and nursed on our soil," and it therefore must be "cleansed" and purged. When Oedipus follows up by asking, "What purification is required?" Creon goes on to interpret the oracle even more specifically, designating the *miasma* to be a punishment for a murder that must be avenged "blood for blood." Finally, to complete this interpretation, Creon informs Oedipus of the unavenged murder of the former king, Laius. This sets the play on its tragic course, as Oedipus, who has saved Thebes once, seeks to save it again, this time by discovering and punishing the murderer, presumably through execution or banishment.

In this sense, and harking back to Camus's Rieux, Oedipus can be said to respond as the perfect "humanist." In a way, he has already shown himself to be this, by solving the riddle of the sphinx — "What goes on four legs in the morning, two legs at noon, and three legs in the evening?" — with the generic and generalizing response, "man." This, of course, is in the myth, not in the play. In the drama, such a general answer will not be enough. Oedipus will have to find the particular individual who committed the murder of Laius. With this translation and interpretation of the words of the oracle, the path of Oedipus's undoing is already determined.

However, there is at least one translator and reader of this play who insisted that this interpretation of the oracle's words, which sets the tragedy in motion, is not the only one possible. This was asserted by Friedrich Hölderlin, who, from 1801–1804, translated both Sophocles's *King Oedipus* and his *Antigone* shortly before suffering a mental breakdown from which he never fully recovered.

Hölderlin accompanied his translations of the two Sophoclean tragedies with "Remarks," the extraordinary density of which has provoked a great number of commentaries. The passage I wish to focus on here begins the second section of his "Remarks on *Oedipus*."[7]

To my knowledge, this section has been largely neglected by critics perhaps because it does not so much discuss the tragedy in its consecrated form, but rather in one that does not exist and probably never could. And yet, Hölderlin nevertheless insists that his remarks seek to articulate nothing less than the key to the work as a whole. It concerns the way Oedipus responds to the words of the oracle. This is how he introduces the remarks: "The *intelligibility* of the whole requires one, above all, to focus on the scene where the oracle's message is *interpreted too infinitely* by Oedipus, tempted by *nefas*."

Hölderlin's use here of the Latin word, *nefas,* is particularly striking, given that he is writing about a Greek tragedy.[8] The word literally means that which is "not said" or should not be said. To write that Oedipus is "tempted by *nefas*" suggests that he yields to the wish to say what is not said and what perhaps is unsayable, and to this end interprets the oracle's words "too infinitely." And yet, when we carefully read Hölderlin's translation of the oracle's message and his gloss of the text, we see that "too infinitely" here also means "too particularly." Here is the passage, first in an English translation, which tries to follow the syntax of Hölderlin's German, rendering Creon's account of the message he brings from the oracle:

> Clearly commanded are we from Phoebus, the king:
> The country's stain (*Schmach*), on this ground nourished,
> Is to be tracked (*verfolgt*), not the incurable nurtured.[9]

There are two main divergences of this Hölderlinian rendering of the oracle from the Watling-Jebb translation: (1) Hölderlin translates *miasma*, which Watling-Jebb render as "unclean thing," as *Schmach*, which I translate as "stain," but which can also mean "disgrace"; (2) Since traditional translations render the oracle as describing the *miasma* as an "unclean thing . . . polluting our soil," the logical response, as already mentioned, is to purge or cleanse it through extirpation. In Hölderlin's translation, by contrast, the oracle commands not to expel the *miasma* but to *verfolgen* — that is, to "track" or "trace" — it. *Verfolgen* can also mean "pursue," but this is still quite different from expelling it, removing it from the place where it was born. This distinction, between expelling and pursuing, allows Hölderlin to introduce the most startling part of his interpretation, not just of the passage, but of the whole tragedy. Note, however, that this surprising gloss is formulated through use of the conditional tense, which gives this interpretation an almost conjectural quality:

> This could mean: judge, generally, a strict and pure tribunal, keep good civic order (*haltet gute bürgerliche Ordnung*). Oedipus, however, responds immediately by speaking in a priestly manner: "Through what cleansing, etc." (731).

Priestly here is linked to the notion of "purgation," "cleansing." To cleanse is to suppose that what needs cleansing is or was originally pure. This assumption of an original purity, which is presumed but not stated as such, is what links the infinite to the finite, the universal to the particular in Oedipus's priestly discourse, as Hölderlin makes clear, when he continues his description of Oedipus' fatal mistake. Having assumed the general necessity of purification, Oedipus then directly moves to *particulars*:

> "And to what man does he signify this destiny?"
>   And it is this that brings Creon's thoughts to the terrible words: "We had, oh king, Laius formerly as lord in this land, before you ruled the city." (731).

To sum up this gloss, Hölderlin interprets Oedipus as yielding to the "temptation" of the *nefas* first by *universalizing* the *miasma* as something that can be purged or "cleansed" and then identifying its cause to be the act of a *particular* individual. Hölderlin elaborates this as follows: "In the following scene, the spirit of Oedipus, all-knowing, speaks out the *nefas* when it suspiciously interprets the [oracle's] general command particularly" (in German: *indem er das allgemeine Gebot argwöhnisch ins Besondere deutet*) by "apply[ing] it to the murderer of Laius, and then tak[ing] the sin to be infinite."[10]

Here, it is not possible to go into the details of this extremely singular and thought-provoking reading. In the context of our previous discussion, concerning the question of recounting plagues, I will simply suggest that Hölderlin's interpretation points to the fact that language, whether oracular or not, inescapably speaks in generalities; and that therefore when it tries to designate particulars, whether an individual murderer or something else, it requires a certain kind of judgment—which some have called a "decision"—in order to make the leap from the general to the particular. Moreover, it is a leap that cannot simply remain within the confines of language. This, perhaps, is why Hölderlin uses here a word in German that designates not simply a self-contained *logical* judgment but an institution, namely *Gericht*. *Gericht* (court, tribunal) includes judgment (*Urteil*) but also goes beyond it, connoting both a relation of forces and a degree of contingency.

The alternative that Hölderlin thus proposes through this reading of Oedipus—the figure and the tragedy—is one that avoids the oracular, the "priestly," and instead is prosaic, or as Hölderlin might have called it, *nüchtern* ("sober"), or in Rieux's words, "modest." It seeks not to "save" but rather only to restore "good civic order." Instead of calling for a savior, it calls for institutions aware of their own enabling limitations—that do not consider themselves either as the material embodiment of general principles or as the instrument of an individual leader.

Instead of "judging priestly" and "too infinitely," the verdicts of such a tribunal could be called "strict and pure" only to the extent that they would not claim to arrive directly at particulars from general concepts or laws. Above all, they would not proceed under the assumption, later formulated by Nietzsche, that "Where there is a deed there must be a doer."[11] What Hölderlin seems to be suggesting, by contrast, is that especially where calamities are concerned, such legalistic and/or monocausal reasoning could be replaced by a decision that would not seek to assign guilt or innocence, but rather to "track" down the structural, social "preexisting conditions" that provide plagues with the indispensable context through which alone they can unleash their destructive force. This could have been what

Hölderlin might have had in mind when he envisaged a response to the oracle that would seek not to identify a murderer but to restore and maintain "good civic order" — *gute bürgerliche Ordnung*.[12] Perhaps.[13]

Of course, had Sophocles allowed Oedipus to respond as envisaged by Hölderlin, we would never have had the tragedy as we know it, nor probably any tragedy at all. Perhaps we would have had something more like a Greek *Trauerspiel* — if such a thing is conceivable (which according to Benjamin it is not). But Hölderlin was not Sophocles, Germany around 1800 was not Athens of 420 BC, and we here today are not either. But Hölderlin's attempt to warn of the danger of responding to catastrophes by confounding the finite with the infinite, the individual with the general, the human with the divine anticipates the lesson that some have learned from the Taiwanese experience with the plague, namely, the need to "foster a discourse of interdependence, [and of] redefining the boundaries between individual choices and civic virtues."

In short, perhaps plagues and calamities can help us to develop practices of solidarity and not simply of solitude, and in so doing, help us not to "forget to be modest."

Covisan

Perhaps it is not entirely inappropriate to close with a brief account of what such a practice of solidarity might look like today, even under the conditions of an order that is highly *bürgerlich*. The program "Covisan" names a project developed first in the Greater Paris area, and as I write, is now being expanded to other parts of France. It involves the use of "mobile teams" that intervene to assist those who have been identified as infected by Covid-19 to help them confront the always singular situation that they thereby have to deal with. The point of the intervention is to break the transmission of the virus not through compulsion, but through assistance in overcoming the specific problems that the "isolation" of infected persons inevitably produces. The project is built on the pioneering work of the French epidemiologist Professor Renaud Piarroux, who developed it first while combatting a cholera epidemic in Haiti. What distinguishes the approach of Professor Piarroux from the more generally repressive measure of general confinement practiced by governments is the effort, as he puts it, "to put oneself in the place of the other, understand his point of view" and try to help the person to confront the problems created by the situation: medical, logistic, economic, psychological.[14]

The aim of Covisan is to encourage solidarity not by trying to impose it through general and repressive measures, but by respecting the specific situations of the singular individuals involved and thus encouraging their participation, rather than provoking their defiance.

Could this also be a model of living not just with plagues, but with each other?

Notes

Textual reference are initially given completely in endnote form, while all following references to the same text are given in-text in parentheses. Wherever possible indications are to sections of the text cited in order to facilitate access independent of the pagination of particular editions. Where foreign words or phrases from the original are cited, references will be both to the English translation and to the foreign edition consulted.

PREFACE

1. Samuel Weber, *Singularity: Politics and Poetics* (Minneapolis, MN: University of Minnesota Press, 2021).

2. Samuel Weber, *The Legend of Freud*, expanded ed. (Stanford, CA: Stanford University Press, 2000), p. 3.

CHAPTER ONE: THE LOCAL AND THE GENERAL

1. A. Wilder-Smith, "Covid-19 in comparison with other emerging viral diseases: risk of geographic spread via travel," *Trop Dis Travel Med Vaccines* 7.3 (2021), https://doi.org/10.1186/s40794-020-00129-9 1.

2. For recent instances of this debate, which call into question the traditional definition of life, see Nigel Brown and David Bhella, "Are Viruses Alive?" *Microbiology Today* 43:2 (May 2016), pp. 58–61; Luis P. Villarreal, "Are Viruses Alive?," *Scientific American* 291:6 (December 2004), pp. 100–105.

3. Latin: *plangere*, Greek: *loimos*, Hebrew: *maggefa* — all suggest a sudden and violent blow. Blows can, of course, be self-inflicted, but this possibility only increases the anxieties produced by the plague, and therefore is difficult to accept.

4. "Recent research has suggested (the) plague first infected humans in Europe and Asia in the Late Neolithic-Early Bronze Age. Research in 2018 found evidence in an ancient Swedish tomb of *Yersinia pestis*, which may have been associated with the 'Neolithic decline' around 3000 BCE, in which European populations fell significantly." "Black Death," Wikipedia, https://en.wikipedia.org/wiki/Black_Death#Previous_plague_epidemics.

5. "Humans are decimating wildlife, and the pandemic is a sign, reports says," *The Washington Post*, September 10, 2020, https://www.washingtonpost.com/science/2020/09/10/wildlife-population-plunge/.

6. Luc Montagnier, whose political history would put him at the opposite end of the spectrum from Trump and Mike Pompeo, strongly suspects that the SARS-CoV-2 virus originated in the Wuhan laboratory, not in the context of developing biological weapons, but far more likely as part of research attempting to develop a vaccine against AIDS. Supporting Montagnier's suspicion is a recent book by an Italian scientist, Professor Joseph Tritto, *Cina Covid-19: La chimera che ha cambiato il mondo* (Siena: Cantagalli, 2020), who, in turn, based his work on that done by two Indian researchers (who subsequently retracted their publication). The hypothesis is based on the discovery of genetic sequences from the HIV virus in SARS-COV-2 and on the argument that the statistical probability of such sequences arising naturally is next to zero. See the interview with Professor Tritto in *France Soir*, August 18, 2020, consultable at: http://www.francesoir.fr/societe-sante/covid-19-lorigine-du-virus-lanalyse-du-pr-tritto-confirme-celle-du-pr-montagnier. For the original paper on which Tritto bases much of his analysis, see Jean-Claude Perez and Luc Montagnier, "COVID-19, SARS and Bats, Corona viruses Genomes Unexpected Exogenous RNA Sequences," OSF Preprints, new manuscript version, June 1, 2020, consultable on the internet: https://osf.io/tgw2d/.

7. Antonin Artaud, "The Theater and the Plague," in *The Theater and Its Double,* trans. Mary Caroline Richards (New York: Grove Press, 1958), p. 16.

8. Albert Camus, *The Plague,* trans. Stewart Gilbert (New York: Vintage International, 1991), p. 245.

9. Walter Benjamin, "The Storyteller," in Howard Eiland (ed.), *Walter Benjamin: Selected Writings, Vol. 3, 1935–1938* (Cambridge, MA: Harvard University Press, 2006), p. 144.

10. Howard Eiland, Michael Jennings, *Walter Benjamin: A Critical Life* (Cambridge, MA: Harvard University Press, 2014), p. 529.

11. "What distinguishes the worst architect from the best of bees is this, that the

architect raises his structure in imagination before he erects it in reality." Karl Marx, *Das Kapital* (Paderborn: Voltmedia, 2005), 1:3 and 1:7 (my translation).

12. Friedrich Nietzsche, *On the Genealogy of Morality and Other Writings*, ed. Keith Ansell-Pearson, trans. Carol Diethe (Cambridge: Cambridge University Press, 2017), book 2, §1.

CHAPTER TWO: MONOTHEOLOGICAL ANTECEDENTS

1. Freud, in his 1915 essay, "Timely thoughts on War and Death," insists that: "One's own death is unimaginable (*unvorstellbar*); and however frequently we attempt it, we discover that we do so as a spectator who survives. Thus, the psychoanalytical School could dare to advance the following proposition: Fundamentally no one believes in their own death; or, what amounts to the same: Unconsciously, every one of us is convinced of our own immortality." Peter Wust, Wilhelm Vernekohl, Augustin Borgolte, et al., eds., *Gesammelte Werke X, Vorlesungen und Briefe* (London: Imago Publishing Co., 1946), p. 341 (my translation).

2. "And when he had called unto [him] his twelve disciples, he gave them power [against] unclean spirits, to cast them out, and to heal all manner of sickness and all manner of disease." Matt. 10:1. See also Matt. 10:8, Mark 3:15, Luke 4:18: "The Spirit of the Lord . . . hath sent me to heal the brokenhearted, to preach deliverance to the captives, and recovering of sight to the blind, to set at liberty them that are bruised."

3. A further emphasis of the importance of the notion of bodily containment is its inversion in regard to these cutaneous eruptions. Defoe describes how physicians desperately attempt to pierce these hardened eruptions and thus to release their deadly fluids, preventing them from entering the bloodstream and leading inevitably to a fatal outcome. Daniel Defoe, *A Journal of the Plague Year*, ed. Paula R. Backscheider (New York: Norton, 1992), p. 137.

4. In the Book of Samuel, Joab's warning reads as follows: "Now the Lord thy God add unto the people, how many soever they be, an hundredfold, and that the eyes of my lord the King may see it: but why doth my lord the King delight in this thing?" (2 Sam. 24:3)

5. *The English Bible: King James Version, Volume One: The Old Testament* (New York: W. W. Norton, 2012), p. 609.

CHAPTER THREE: POLYTHEISTIC ANTECEDENTS

1. In March of 2020, as Covid-19 began to spread rapidly in Europe and France, the French President, Emmanuel Macron, declared (six times in a single speech), that "We are at war" ("Nous sommes en guerre"), albeit against an "invisible and intangible enemy"

(un "ennemi […] invisible, insaisissable"). "'Nous sommes en guerre': face au coronavirus, Emmanuel Macron sonne la 'mobilisation générale,'" *Le Monde*, March 17, 2020, consulted at: https://www.lemonde.fr/politique/article/2020/03/17/nous-sommes-en-guerre-face-au-coronavirus-emmanuel-macron-sonne-la-mobilisation-generale_6033338_823448.html. A day later President Donald Trump tweeted "The world is at war with a hidden enemy. WE WILL WIN." https://twitter.com/realdonaldtrump/status/1239997820242923521.

2. For a recent discussion of the history and contemporary problems in maintaining and developing such "rules of war," see the following transcript of keynote address by Peter Maurer and panel discussion with Susan Glasser, Peter Maurer, J. Stephen Morrison, and Charles ("Cully") Stimson: "Rules in War — A Thing of the Past?," CSIS (Center for Strategic and International Studies), May 10, 2019, https://www.csis.org/analysis/rules-war-thing-past.

3. Carl Schmitt, *Theory of the Partisan*, trans. G. L. Ulmen (New York: Telos Press, 2007).

4. See the so-called Yan Report, largely dismissed by the mainstream media, but rarely discussed in any detail. What is significant in my view is that the claims being made by the authors are exaggerated in order to justify the dismissal. They claim that there is reason to warrant an "independent international investigation," not that they have proved anything. However, it is the latter that is imputed to them by those who would close off the possibility of investigation and discussion. It seems as if the report is no longer accessible on the internet (as of September 20, 2020). The Twitter account of the author was cancelled within forty-eight hours of the publication of the report. The proximity of the authors to Steve Bannon and other figures close to the Trump administration suffices here, as in the case of hydroxychloroquine, to preempt serious consideration of the arguments and available data. A further, more detailed, report is promised by the author and her team. It remains to be seen if they will be able to transmit it. More recently, Dr. Alina Chan, a Canadian microbiologist, testified before a Parliamentiary committee "that a leak from a laboratory in Wuhan region of China is now the 'more likely' origin of the Covid-19 global pandemic," ndtv.com/world-news/coronavirus-wuhan-lab-leak-more-likely-origin-of-covid-19-says-researcher-2653379. For an overview of the controversy, recent at the time of this writing, see: Richard Horton, "Offline: The origin story — division deepens" (December 18, 2021), https://www.thelancet.com/journals/lancet/article/PIIS0140-6736(21)02833-6/fulltext.

5. This same anxiety is probably one of the major forces behind the growing attraction of conspiracy theories: a conspiracy is evidence not just of a malevolent (or benevolent)

group working out of sight to influence events, but more generally a confirmation of the capacity of human intelligence and effort to control an uncertain and possibly danger-ous future — a future that for many seems especially frightening because it is out of the control of the established institutions, which are increasingly discrediting themselves by demonstrating their inability to respond effectively to challenges, such as Covid-19. This is by no means true everywhere — confidence in national leadership has actually risen in certain countries as a result of their handling of the pandemic — but it seems true in a very large number of areas.

6. Given the system of alliances that constituted both the Athenian "empire" and the Spartan league, the distinction between interstate and civil war is not always easy to maintain or discern, as we shall see shortly. In politics, as elsewhere, the distinction between "internal" and "external" is never absolute. Thucydides, *History of the Pelopon-nesian War,* trans. Rex Warner (New York: Penguin Books, 1972). Unless otherwise indi-cated all quotes are from the Warner translation.

7. Thucydides, *The Landmark Thucydides,* ed. Robert B. Strassler (New York: Free Press, 1996), p. 112 based on a newly revised edition of the Richard Crowley translation.

8. Gregory Nagy, "The Subjectivity of Fear as Reflected in Ancient Greek Wording," The Center for Hellenic Studies, November 2, 2020, http://nrs.harvard.edu/urn-3:hlnc. essay:Nagy.The_Subjectivity_of_Fear.2010.

9. The plague of Athens, which is today considered to have probably been a version of typhus, is estimated to have killed from one-fourth to one-third of the population of Athens. It lasted, off and on, from 430 to 426 BC. "Peste d'Athènes," Wikipédia, https:// fr.wikipedia.org/wiki/Peste_d%27Athènes.

10. Michael Loriaux, to whom much in this chapter is indebted, argues that for Thucydides, the Athenians are prisoners of the *pleonexia* and *anomie* that enabled their imperialism, and sees here a possible "flaw in *physis* itself." I am not sure that I would ascribe the kind of universality associated with "*physis*" to this phenomenon, however widespread it undoubtedly is and has been. My tendency would be to see the desire to expand and "have more" as a response rather than an inborn natural trait. If *pleonexia* is the desire to have more — than the other, than what one is due, etc. — then it is responding, defensively and aggressively, to a sense of lack that from a Lacanian point of view could be characterized as "imaginary": the other is the model of perfection, of the norm, but as other is unattainable to a self (*moi*) that experiences itself as incomplete and deficient, and so must seek to exceed itself and-or deprive the other or both. Hence, Pericles is "right"

when he tells the Athenians that they are trapped in their own imperialist successes and excesses — because the latter are already a response to a sense of being entrapped in one's inadequacies or limitations. Can one relate to limitation other than as a "lack" to be supplanted or suppressed? Or put differently, can there be a sense of self that can accommodate limitation rather than trying to eliminate it? This is one of the questions that plagues and pandemics pose not just to individuals but to societies.

11. Of course, mortality is quite calculable from the point of view of large numbers, groups, etc., but in its irreducible relation to the singular living being, it remains never entirely calculable — which is why Pericles, in his discourse, is so quick to transcend the individual experience and proceed to the general, collective one.

12. See the Spartan judgment of the Plataeans, 3:52–68, and Nicias's "addiction" to divination, 7:50, as well as descriptions of his character in general (with thanks to Michael Loriaux for pointing out these passages to me).

CHAPTER FOUR: STORYTELLING AS FRICTION

1. I follow here and throughout the excellent introduction by Wayne Rebhorn to his translation of Giovanni Boccaccio, *The Decameron* (Norton Critical Editions), trans. Wayne A. Rebhorn (New York: W. W. Norton, 2016), p. xxi.

2. See Rebhorn, who remarks that "the storytellers do assemble in a real place, the Church of Santa Maria Novella, which was probably chosen because the last word in its name looks forward to the stories, the novelle, they would be telling" (Rebhorn, *The Decameron*, p. xxii). One could add that the Church in which they meet is described by Boccaccio as "venerable" but also as "otherwise almost empty" (Rebhorn, *The Decameron*, p. 11). Whether this is because of the plague or not, there is the suggestion that the *novella* of the Catholic Church has lost much of its power and attraction, and in the space thus opened up, the "novelle" that will compose the *Decameron* take place — without attempting to present themselves as elements of a new religion of art. Historically, that will come later, but Boccaccio's fictions have a "frictional" relation to reality, since they bring out its internal conflicts and contradictions, while suggesting alternatives not so much in the content of what they tell as in the telling itself.

3. With respect to the relation of "friction" to "frame" as they concern literature, the study of Simone Heller-Andrist, *The Friction of the Frame: Derrida's Parergon in Literature* (Tübingen: Francke Verlag, 2012) stands out as one of the very few to explore this motif. However, despite mentioning the word "friction" in her title, her study focuses almost

entirely on the Derridean notion of "the frame" in its "parergonal" aspect and has very little to say about its frictional aspect.

4. "No hard evidence exists that Boccaccio was actually in Florence when the plague broke out — indeed, there are records of Boccaccio's having been in the town of Forli in late 1347 and early 1348 — and many elements in his description of the ravages of the disease come from the eighth-century *Historia Longobardorum* (History of the Lombards) by Paulus Diaconus. However, his father, who was the minister of supply and was in charge of organizing relief during the epidemic, may have communicated details about the disaster to him" (Rebhorn, *Decameron*, p. xviii). This is, as we shall see, similar to the situation of Defoe, who establishes himself as fictional eyewitness based probably on information given him by his uncle, since he was a child at the time of the Great Plague of London in 1665.

5. Note how Boccaccio "adds insult to injury" here by noting that it is not husbands who abandon their wives but the other way around, thus pointing to the way in which the plague disrupts the usual hierarchical relation that makes wives dependent upon their husbands.

6. Shame is also what Adam and Eve feel when they are accosted by God after having transgressed his prohibition to eat of the tree of the knowledge of good and evil. Shame remains the feeling most closely allied with guilt at having violated the laws that support hierarchies — whether that between the human and the divine, or as here, the relation between the sexes. Shame involves both the response to being "caught" in the act of such violation, as well as the acknowledgement of guilt. Its Biblical heritage of being associated with death is here both confirmed and transformed, since it opens the possibility of a new form of life "in the period that followed."

7. Jacques Derrida, "Et cetera," in *Derrida*, eds. Marie-Louise Mallet and Ginette Michaud (Paris: Éditions de l'Herne, 2004), p. 21.

8. Rebhorn, *Decameron*, p. 331, n.9.

9. Benjamin, "The Storyteller," p. 146.

CHAPTER FIVE: THE LUTHERAN RESPONSE

1. Martin Luther, "Ob man vor dem Sterben fliehen möge" (1552), in *Ausgewählte Schriften*, vol. 2, ed. Hans Christian Knuth (Frankfurt am Main: Insel Verlag, 2016), p. 225. English quotes of Luther refer to: Martin Luther, "Whether One May Flee From a Deadly Plague" (1527), in *Luther's Works*, vol. 43, *Devotional Writings*, ed. Gustav K. Wiencke, trans. Carl J. Schindler (Philadelphia, PA: Fortress Press, 1968). After the initial citation reference in an endnote, future references to the same work are given in the body of the text.

2. Peter Blickle, *Communal Reformation. The Quest for Salvation in Sixteenth-Century Germany*, trans. Thomas Dunlap, Studies in Central European Histories 1 (Atlantic Highlands, NJ: Humanities Press, 1992), p. 154, cited by Dean Philip Bell in his informative article on Luther's response to the plague, "Ministry and Sacred Obligation: A Late Medieval Context for Luther's 'On Whether One May Flee from the Death,'" in Christine Helmer, ed., *The Medieval Luther* (Tübingen: Siebeck, 2020), pp. 197–212. I am indebted to Christine Helmer for acquainting me with this publication and for her extensive and very helpful comments on this chapter.

3. These attacks were nothing new, since already the pogroms in the thirteenth century were justified by the belief that the Jews were poisoning the water. See "Persecution of Jews during the Black Death," Wikipedia, https://en.wikipedia.org/wiki/Persecution_of_Jews_during_the_Black_Death; and regarding Luther's tract: "On the Jews and Their Lies," Wikipedia, https://en.wikipedia.org/wiki/On_the_Jews_and_Their_Lies.

CHAPTER SIX: "OUT OF ALL MEASURES"

1. Daniel Defoe, *A Journal of the Plague Year*, ed. Paula R. Backscheider (New York: Norton, 1992), p. ix. Future references to this work will be given in parentheses in the body of the text.

2. In the case of *Moll Flanders,* the text is presented by an editor as a cleaned-up version of an originally autobiographical account, in which the indecorous language has been modified for more general and polite consumption.

3. Rom. 14:7. See above, p. 127.

4. Michel Foucault, *Discipline and Punish: The Birth of the Prison* (New York: Vintage Books, 1977), pp. 195–200.

CHAPTER SEVEN: TRAGEDY AS *TRAUERSPIEL*

1. Heinrich von Kleist, *Robert Guiskard: Herzog der Normänner*, ed. Carlos Spoerhase (Stuttgart: Reclam, 2011), p. 37 (my translation). Future citations from this play will be given in the text, with "R" for Reclam and the page number.

2. Quoted in the excellent afterword (*Nachwort*) by Spoerhase in *Robert Guiskard.*

3. G. A. Loud, *The Age of Robert Guiscard: Southern Italy and the Norman Conquest* (Harlow: Pearson Education Limited, 2000), p. 223.

4. Loud, *Age of Robert Guiscard*, p. 3.

5. Friedrich Hölderlin, "Oedipus," in *Hölderlin's Sophocles: Oedipus and Antigone*, trans.

David Constantine (Highgreen, Tarset: Bloodaxe Books, 2001), p. 17 (translation modified).

6. For philological accuracy, it should be noted that *Oedipus Tyrannos* and *Oedipus at Colonus* were written at different times and therefore do not stand in direct relation to one another.

7. Heinrich von Kleist, *Five Plays*, trans. and intro. Martin Greenberg (New Haven, CT: Yale University Press, 1988), p. 353. Future references to this edition will be given in parentheses in the text preceded by G (for Greenberg). A second English translation, by L. R. Scheuer, will also occasionally be used: "Robert Guiscard, Duke of the Normans: Fragment of a Tragedy," *Tulane Drama Review* 6.3 (March 1962), pp. 178–92. Stable URL: https://www.jstor.org/stable/1124943). Page numbers will be preceded by S. English translations quoted are modified throughout.

8. Walter Benjamin, *Origin of the German Trauerspiel*, trans. Howard Eiland (Cambridge, MA: Harvard University Press, 2019), p. 72.

9. In a curious way, this representation of Abelard, questioning the legitimacy of blood ties in the transmission of power, links up with the "frame" in which I, and some others, read Sophocles's Oedipus. Oedipus is, of course, the hereditary heir of the throne of Thebes, although he does not know it. But the curse on Laertes prohibits such hereditary transmission of power. And Oedipus's end at Colonus recognizes, through the figure of Theseus, that the security and survival of a polity may depend more on the non-hereditary transmission of power than on military force. For the non-hereditary transmission of power can converge with a respect for the other, for the foreigner, that can be the key to the survival of a political entity — which otherwise, as with Thebes, threatens to implode by virtue of inbreeding. The plague in *Oedipus Tyrannos* can be interpreted in this way. See my reading of it in Samuel Weber, *Theatricality as Medium* (New York: Fordham University Press, 2004), pp. 103–10 and 141–59.

10. Daniel Defoe, *A Journal of the Plague Year*, ed. Paula R. Backscheider (New York: Norton, 1992), p. 184.

CHAPTER EIGHT: PREEXISTING CONDITIONS

1. Anaïs Nin, *The Diary of Anaïs Nin, vol. 1, 1931–1934,* ed. Gunther Stuhlmann (Boston, MA: Mariner Books, 1969), p. 192. After the initial citation reference in an endnote, future references to the same work are given in the body of the text.

2. Nin, *Diary*, p. 193.

3. Antonin Artaud, "The Theater and the Plague," in *The Theater and Its Double,* trans.

Mary Caroline Richards (New York: Grove Press, 1958), p. 32.

4. See Elena Scappaticci, "Hilter, son psy, son amante . . . Les 'lettres-sort' d'Antonin Artaud aux enchères," *Le Figaro*, January 11, 2017, https://www.lefigaro.fr/culture/encheres/2017/01/11/03016-20170111ARTFIG00380-hitler-son-psy-son-amante-les-lettres-sort-d-antonin-artaud-aux-encheres.php.

5. Foucault, *Discipline and Punish*, pp. 197–98. Needless to say, the increase in regulations imposed by governments in their attempt to control the spread of Covid-19 raises similar issues, although there is little or no attempt to endorse the "literary fiction" of the plague as a kind of "festival."

6. For a long time, it seemed as if the success of Taiwan in controlling the spread of Covid-19 could be seen as a confirmation of the viceroy's decision as recounted by Artaud. Without having to resort to widespread "lockdowns," Taiwan was able to control the spread of the virus through the speed and coordination with which it applied protective measures: controlling borders, testing, tracing, and isolating. However, starting in May of 2021, the virus began to spread, for a variety of reasons. One of which was its initial success, which encouraged overconfidence and reduced observance of "social distancing." See: Yvette Tan, "Covid-19: What went wrong in Singapore and Taiwan?" BBC News, May 20, 2021 https://www.bbc.com/news/world-asia-57153195.

7. Wikipédia, "Peste de Marseille (1720)," https://fr.wikipedia.org/wiki/Peste_de_Marseille_(1720)#Causes_de_la_propagation_et_type_de_peste. "It is probable that interventions occurred so that the least strict regulations were applied. It is impossible to know the persons really involved, but the convergence of the interests of the families of merchants and of the authorities who ruled the city is sufficient to explain the numerous negligences" (my translation).

8. This text and performance, originally planned to be broadcast on French radio on February 1, 1948, but which was then censored, can be consulted on YouTube: https://www.youtube.com/watch?v=EXy7lsGNZ5A.

9. Martin Heidegger, *Identity and Difference*, trans. Joan Stambaugh (Chicago, IL: University of Chicago Press, 2002).

10. Luther, see above, p. 97.

11. Boccaccio, *The Decameron* (Norton Critical Editions), trans. Wayne A. Rebhorn (New York: W. W. Norton, 2016), pp. 6–7.

12. It can be noted that English preserves the distinction Artaud is driving toward here in the differentiation it makes between "acting" and "action," between "actor" and

"active": the former remain "enclosed," as it were, in themselves, and in that sense remain virtual, not "real." But this self-enclosed virtuality opens up their signifying force in precisely the way Artaud is suggesting.

13. "When the consciousness of the latent presence of violence in a legal institution disappears, the institution falls into decay. In our time, parliaments provide an example of this. They offer the familiar, woeful spectacle because they have not remained conscious of the revolutionary forces to which they owe their existence." Walter Benjamin, "Toward a Critique of Violence," in *Selected Writings*, eds. Marcus Bullock and Michael W. Jenning, vol. 1, 1913–1926 (Cambridge, MA: Harvard University Press, 1996), p. 244.

14. Defoe, *Journal,* p. 69.

15. Artaud's description here recalls the remarks of certain physicians concerning the thickening and clotting of the blood produced by Covid-19.

16. In Defoe's London, much of what Artaud describes applies, but not the collapse of the municipal administration, which despite the Royal Court absconding to Oxford, continues to function and to take measures to contain the plague and its effects. However, as in Artaud's description, there is "no army" available, which is another reason Defoe lauds the social measures taken by the city government to alleviate the situation of the poor, thus avoiding a possible revolt.

17. It should not be overlooked that the English translation renders the French word *esprit* variously as "spirit" and as "mind," thus somewhat weakening its Christian heritage.

CHAPTER NINE: CONFINEMENT

1. Albert Camus, *The Plague,* trans. Stuart Gilbert (New York: Vintage Books, 1991), p. 91. Future references to this edition given in the body of text, followed by references to the French edition, *La Peste* (Paris: Gallimard, 1947).

2. Camus, *La Peste,* p. 7. The English publication omits the epigraph.

3. Roland Barthes, "*La Peste:* annales d'une épidémie ou roman de la solitude?" *Club* (Bulletin du Club du Meilleur Livre, January, 1955), reprinted in: *Roland Barthes, Œuvres complètes*, ed. Éric Marty, vol. 1, 1942–1961 (Paris: Seuil, 2002), p. 541. Quotes from Barthes and Camus's response are my translations.

4. Cited by Michel Murat, "La peste comme analogie," *fabula*, atelier de théorie littéraire, May 2020, https://www.fabula.org/atelier.php?La_peste_comme_analogie.

5. In an early manuscript, Camus filled in the date, giving it as 1941, which, however, he later changed. There was small outbreak of bubonic plague in Oran in 1945, following

a more serious one in Algiers the previous year. But nothing on the scale described in the novel, which was published in 1947.

6. Edward Said asks: "Why was Algeria a setting for narratives whose main reference (in the case of the first two) has always been construed as France generally and, more particularly, France under the Nazi Occupation?" Edward Said, *Culture and Imperialism* (New York: Vintage, 1994), p. 224. The responses he provides, however, are far less helpful for *The Plague* than for *The Stranger*. Unfortunately, Said has the tendency to confound the two, as the following assertion indicates: "Both *l'Etranger* and *La Peste* are about the deaths of Arabs." Whereas the murder of an Arab is at the core of the plot of *The Stranger*, there are significantly no such scenes described in *The Plague*. Conor Cruise O'Brien is much closer to the text when he observes that "having provided [an] occasion for the demonstration of integrity [of Dr. Rieux], the Arabs of Oran absolutely cease to exist." Conor Cruise O'Brien, *Camus* (London: Faber & Faber, 2015), Kindle edition, p. 46. He concludes, "The native question is simply abolished." It is precisely this abolition and its replacement by the plague that will concern us in the following pages.

7. For this information as for so much else concerning the novel and its background, I am greatly indebted to the memoir of Denis Guénoun, "Oran et *La Peste*" (Oran and the Plague), *fabula*, atelier de théorie littéraire (originally published on April 12, 2020 on https://denisguenoun.org/), https://www.fabula.org/atelier.php?Oran_Camus_la_peste.

8. Herbert Lottmann, *Albert Camus: A Biography* (Corte Madera, CA: Gingko Press, 2013), Kindle edition, location 6206.

9. This narrative "exclusion of exclusion" corresponds closely to the function of what Freud, in *The Interpretation of Dreams*, calls "secondary revision" or "elaboration." Secondary revision "revises" or reworks the distorted, conflictual subtext of the dream (its "latent content") so that it appears to correspond to the demands of waking (self-)consciousness. Despite or rather because of its apparent coherence, it can be seen as a "distortion of a distortion." The form this usually takes is the construction of a causally coherent, continuous narrative. Camus's novel can be interpreted as doing something very similar with respect to the conflictual subtext of colonial exclusion and subordination. As we will see, however, Camus's "secondary revision" is by no means fully unconscious or total: it allows the excluded to appear between the lines and on the margins, as it were. For an interpretation of "secondary revision" in this sense, see Samuel Weber, *Legend of Freud* (Stanford, CA: Stanford University Press, 2000), pp. 40–47.

10. Wikipedia, "French Algeria," https://en.wikipedia.org/wiki/French_Algeria. It

should be noted that one month before the publication of *La Peste*, Camus denounced the massacres of 1945 in an article published in *Combat* in May of 1947. See Albert Camus, in *Œuvres complètes*, ed. Jacqueline Lévi-Valensi, vol. 2 (Paris: Gallimard, Bibliothèque de la Pléiade, 2006), pp. 429–31.

11. This recalls the moving and shocking testimony of a nurse from South Dakota, who, toward the end of November 2020, recounted that certain of her patients who were dying of Covid-19 refused to the end to believe that their disease was real. "Nurse: Some patients who test positive refuse to believe they have Covid-19," interview by Alisyn Camerota, New Day, November 16, 2020, *CNN*, https://edition.cnn.com/videos/us/2020/11/16/south-dakota-nurse-intv-newday-vpx.cnn. Her account is a grim confirmation of Artaud's observation that "the mind believes what it sees and does what it believes" (Artaud, "The Theater and the Plague," p. 27).

CHAPTER TEN: LIVING WITH PLAGUES

1. "The Plague is not so much a novel as a sermon in the form of a fable." Conor Cruise O'Brien, *Camus* (London: Faber & Faber, 2015), Kindle edition, p. 43.

2. Of course, the familiarity of such associations depends heavily on specific cultural and historical conditions, something that Camus does not sufficiently take into account. Here, through his character, he conflates individualism, capitalism, and (Christian) humanism and then universalizes the amalgam.

3. Auriane Guilbaud, Philippe Sansonetti, et al., *Le retour des épidémies* (Paris: Presses Universitaires de France, 2015).

4. On the changing situation in Taiwan, see above p. 170.

5. Ming-Cheng M. Lo and Hsin-Yi Hsieh, "The 'Societalization' of Pandemic Unpreparedness: Lessons from Taiwan's COVID Response," *American Journal of Cultural Sociology* 8 (Sept. 19, 2020), pp. 384–404, https://doi.org/10.1057/s41290-020-00113-y.

6. It can also mean "stain," "defilement." Henry George Liddell and Robert Scott, *An Intermediate Greek-English Lexicon* (Oxford: Clarendon Press, 1975), p. 512.

7. Two English translations of Hölderlin's "Remarks" are available: Friedrich Hölderlin, *Essays and Letters on Theory*, trans. and ed. Thomas Pfau (Albany, NY: State University of New York Press, 1988), pp. 101–16, and *Hölderlin's Sophocles*, trans. David Constantine (Highgreen, Tarset: Bloodaxe Books, 2001), pp. 63–68, 113–18. I have consulted both but used my own translations. For the German see: Friedrich Hölderlin, *Werke und Briefe*, eds. Friedrich Beissner and Jochen Schmidt, vol. 2 (Frankfurt: Insel Verlag, 1969), pp. 729–36, 783–90.

8. The word does occur several times in his previous unsuccessful attempt to write a tragedy on Empedocles.

9. In German: "Geboten hat uns Phöbus klar, der König,/Man soll des Landes Schmach, auf diesem Grund genährt,/Verfolgen, nicht Unheilbares ernähren." Hölderlin, *Werke und Briefe 2*, p. 731 (my translation).

10. Hölderlin, *Werke und Briefe 2*, p. 732.

11 Nietzsche, *Genealogy of Morals,* book 1, §13. In German, Nietzsche uses the word *Täter*, which ordinarily means not "doer," as usually rendered in English, but "culprit," "perpetrator," thus introducing the attribution of "guilt" and hence the presupposition not just of subjective "agency" but of a preexisting legal framework that takes for granted the "applicability" of the general "law" to the singular "deed."

12. Hölderlin, *Werke und Briefe 2*, p. 731.

13. "Perhaps! But who is willing to care about such dangerous 'perhapses'?" Friedrich Nietzsche, *Beyond Good and Evil* (Cambridge: Cambridge University Press, 2001), book 1, §2. In this particular context, the question to be asked is to what extent the two adjectives used by Hölderlin here, namely, *gute* and *bürgerliche* are compatible—given that the latter term designates not simply "civic" as I have rendered it, but also "bourgeois"? If, as might be argued, a "bourgeois" order is one that is ruled by the *universal* equivalent of money and exchange value, then what makes a social order "good" is inseparable from its ability to respect the irreducibility of *singular differences*.

14. Laureline Dubuy, "Renaud Piarroux: un épidémiologiste de terrain contre le Covid-19," *La Croix*, December 12, 2020, https://www.la-croix.com/Sciences-et-ethique /Renaud-Piarroux-epidemiologiste-terrain-contre-Covid-19-2020-12-16-1201130473.Pier-roux is the author of two books (in French) recounting his experiences: *Cholera: Haïti 2010–2018: histoire d'un désastre* (Paris: Editions du CNRS, 2019) and *La vague. L'épidémie vu du terrain* (Paris: Editions du CNRS, 2020). For Covisan, see Apolline Rouze, "Covisan: une prise en charge à domicile des patients Covid," *Pôle Santé Paris 13*, May 26, 2020, https://www.polesante13.fr/blog/1/post/covisan-une-prise-en-charge-a-domicile-des -patients-covid-21. For two brief accounts in English: https://www.france24.com /en/video/20200526-french-hospitals-deploy-mobile-teams-to-track-and-trace-covid-19 -cases, and https://www.dw.com/en/frances-covid-19-brigades-fighting-the-virus-at -what-cost/a-53656664.

Index